Natural Musings

Photography and Poetry

Volume 1

By Michelle R.K. Hed

For Paul, Mikayla and Samantha ~
Thank you for your unending patience while I spent hours on my computer writing poetry, for accompanying me on photographic journeys and for giving me your unconditional love and support.

Summer

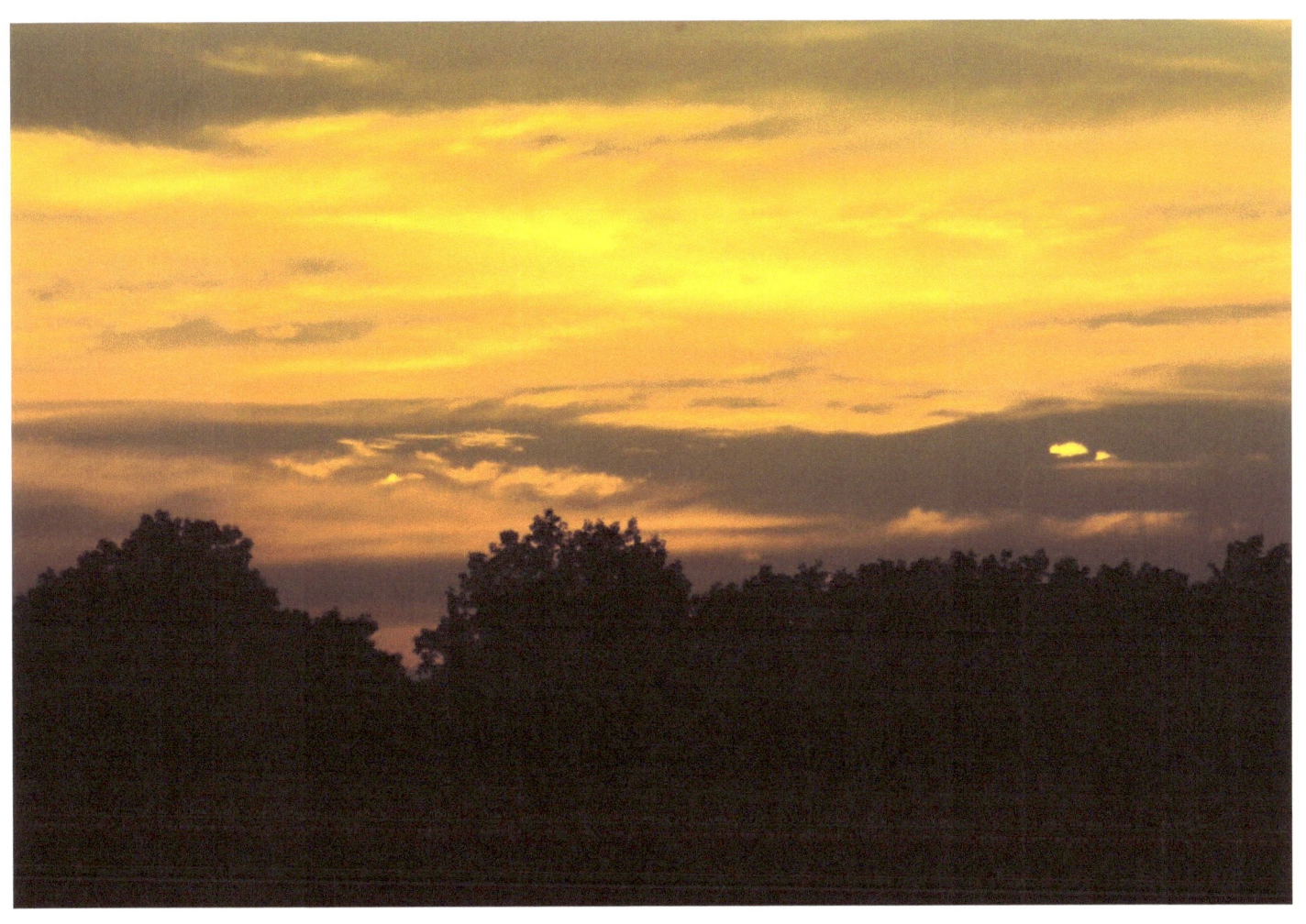

on dewy grass
watching the sunrise
God paints

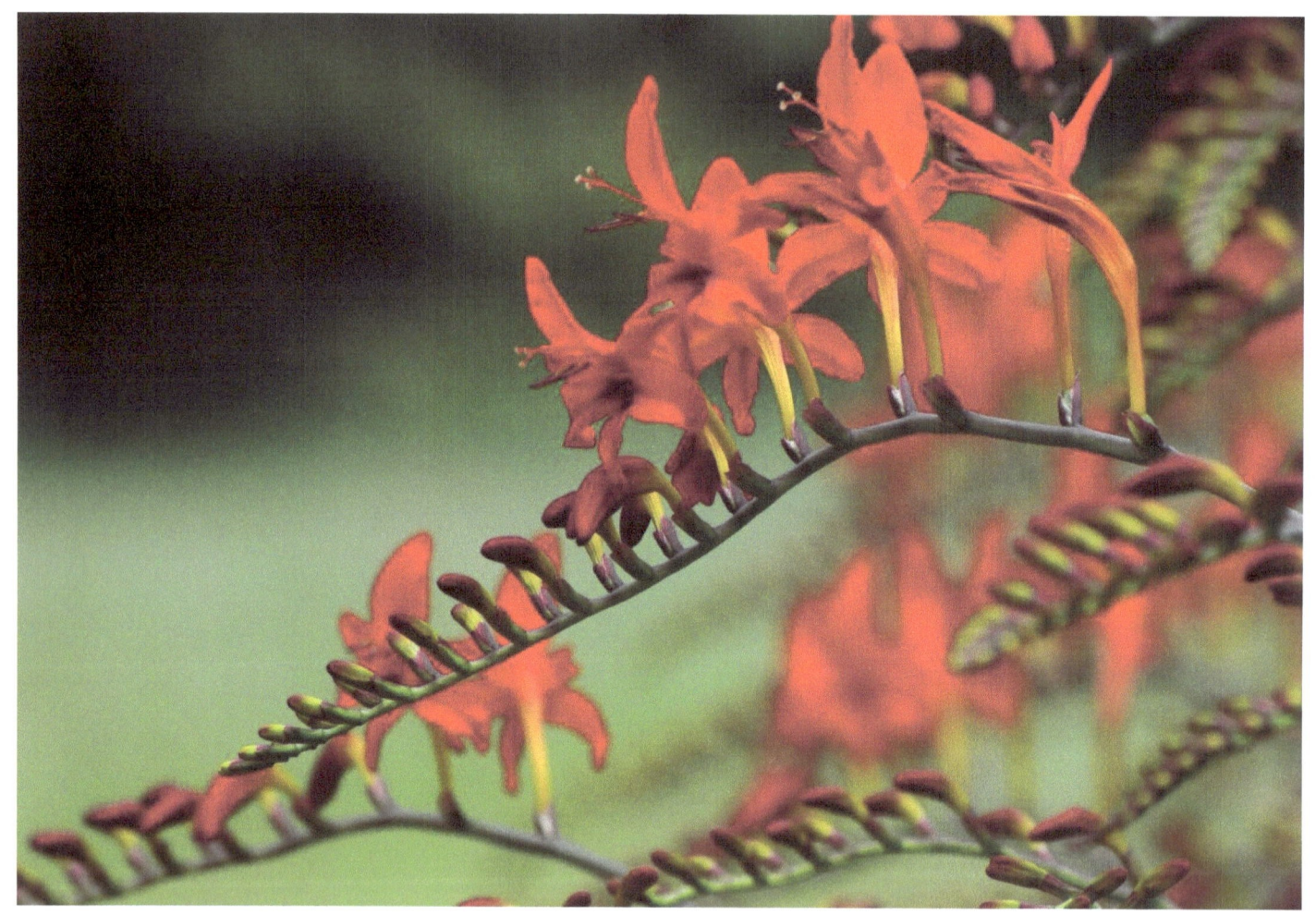

Lucifer Crocosmia

tiny red-hot flames
dance along the stalk
opening with the heat of the sun

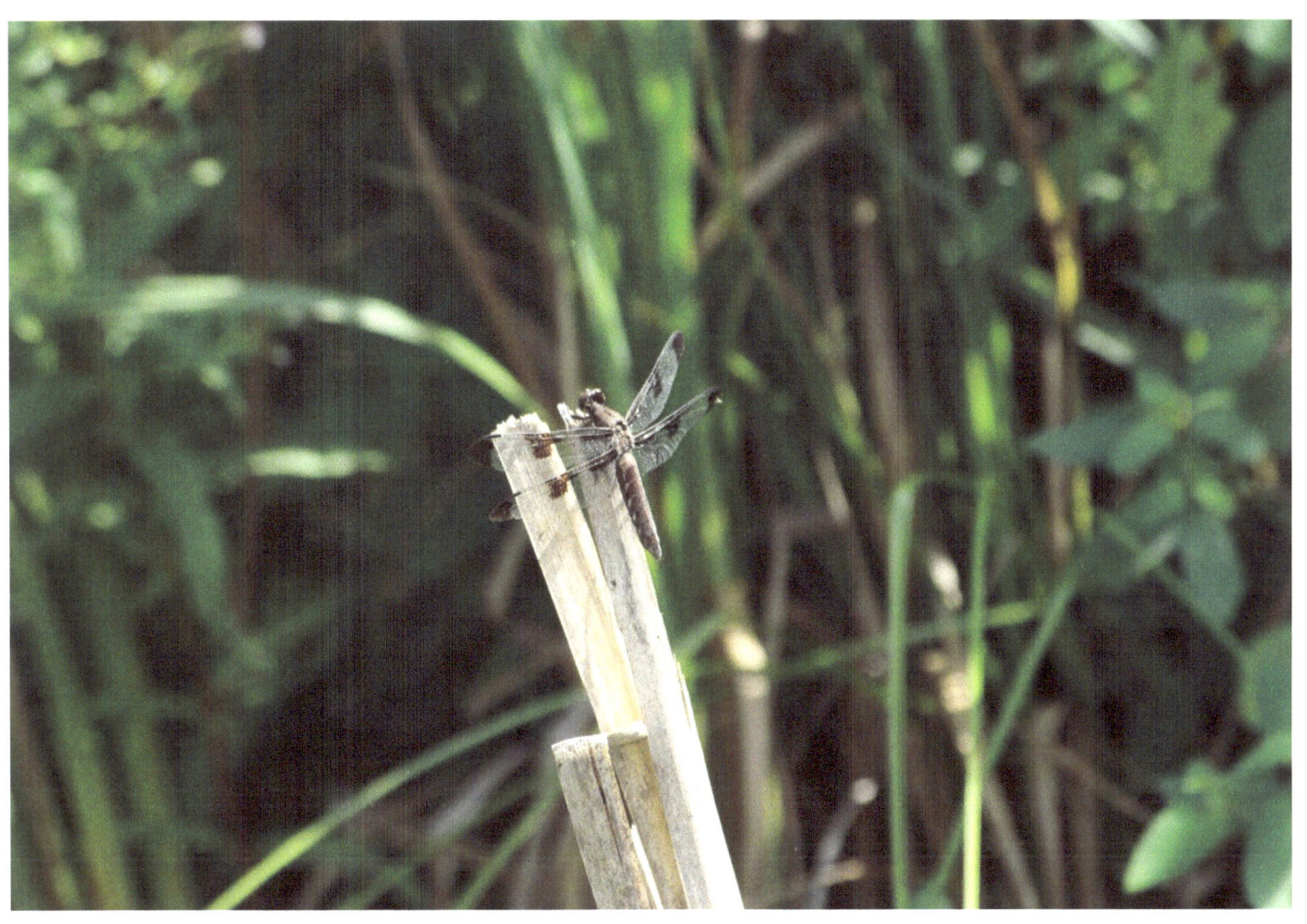

patterns in the lines
of transparent wings -
nature's fine art

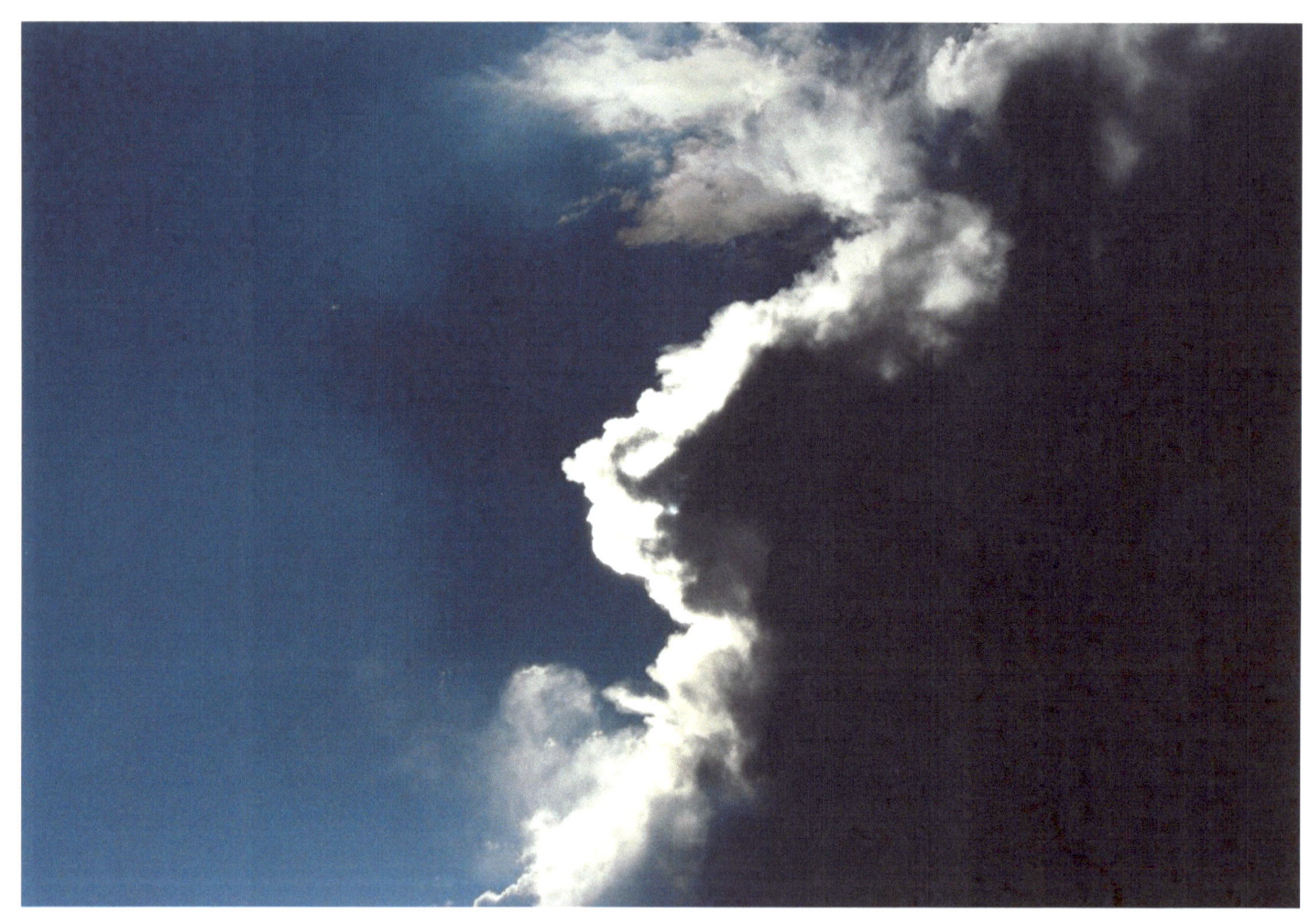

sun hiding
storm clouds rolling
glimpse of God's silhouette

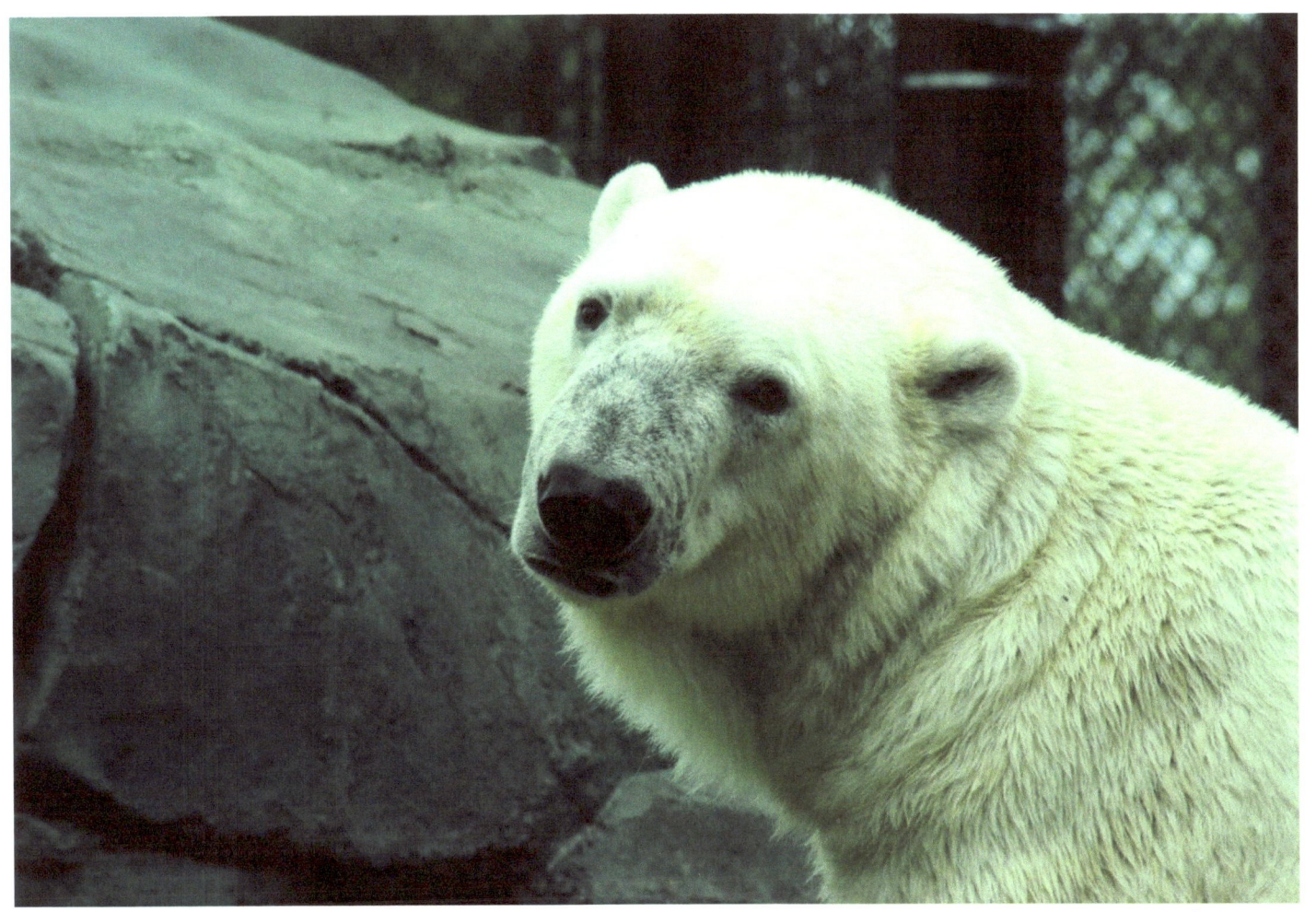

Polar Bear – Como Zoo, St. Paul, MN

watching your ice cream drip
he stares –
leapfrogging ice floes

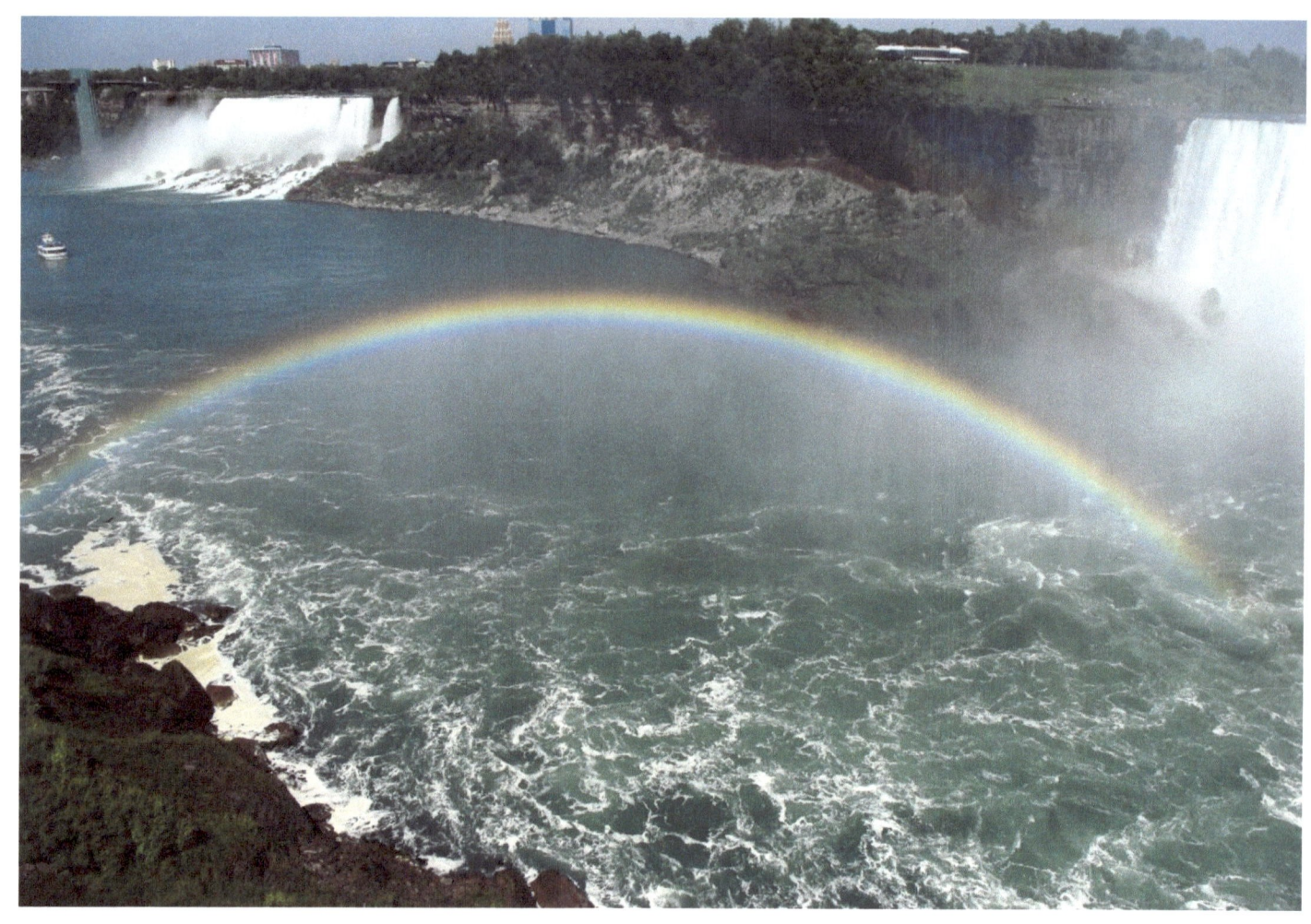

over the water
a rainbow stretched -
gold beneath the crests

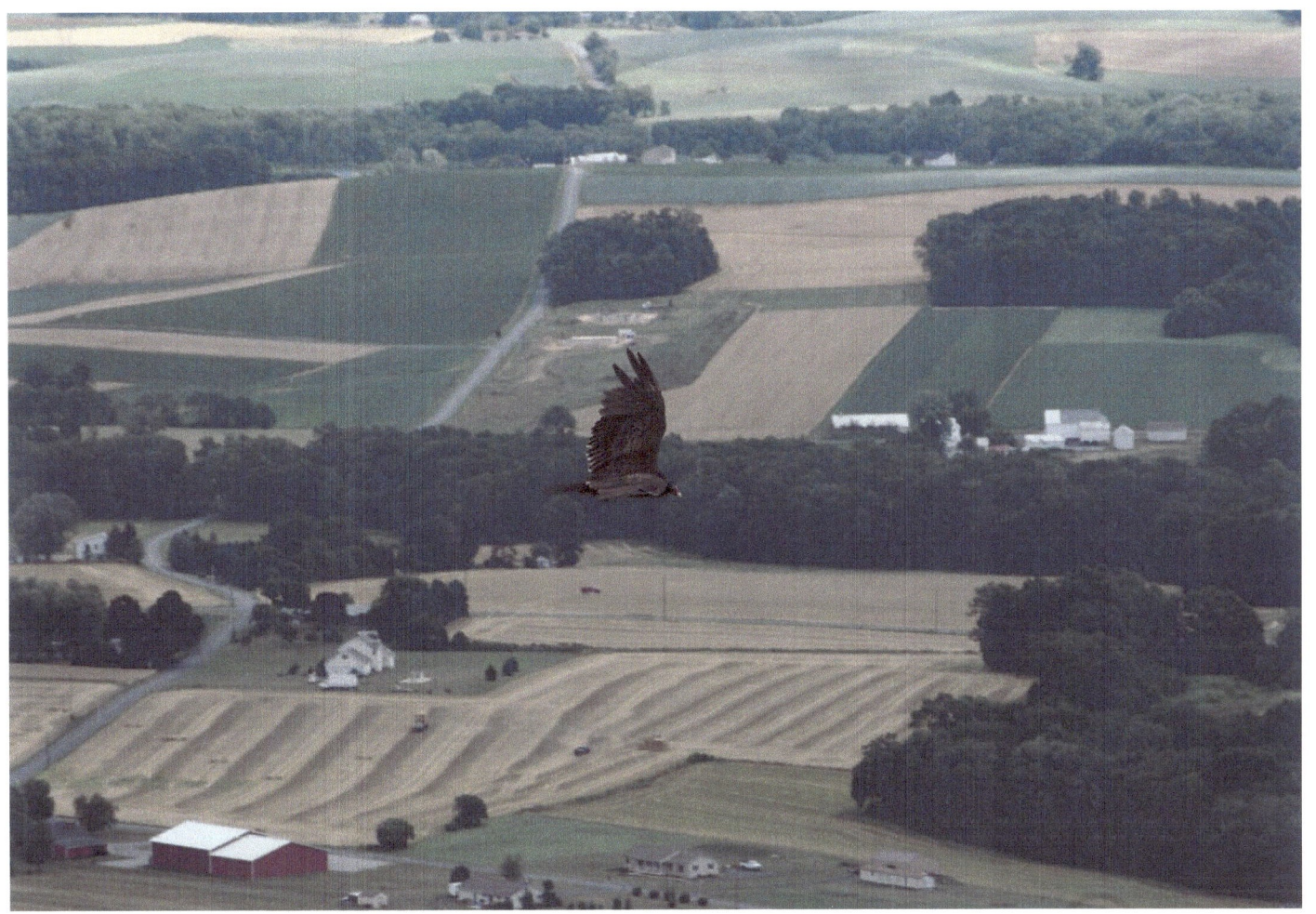

Turkey Vulture

hiking the Appalachian Trail
my heart soars
far above the valley

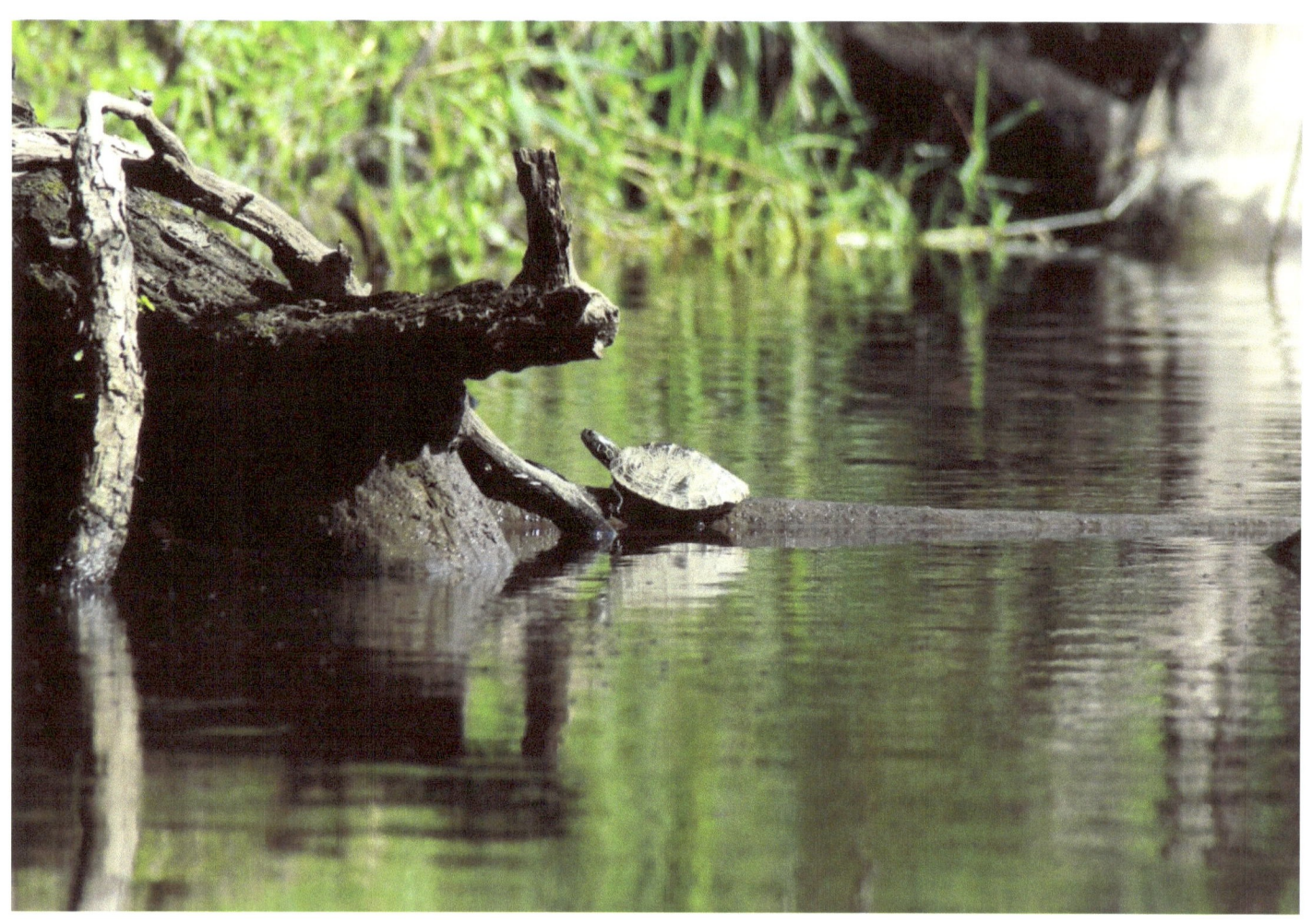

water reflects life
moveable canvas

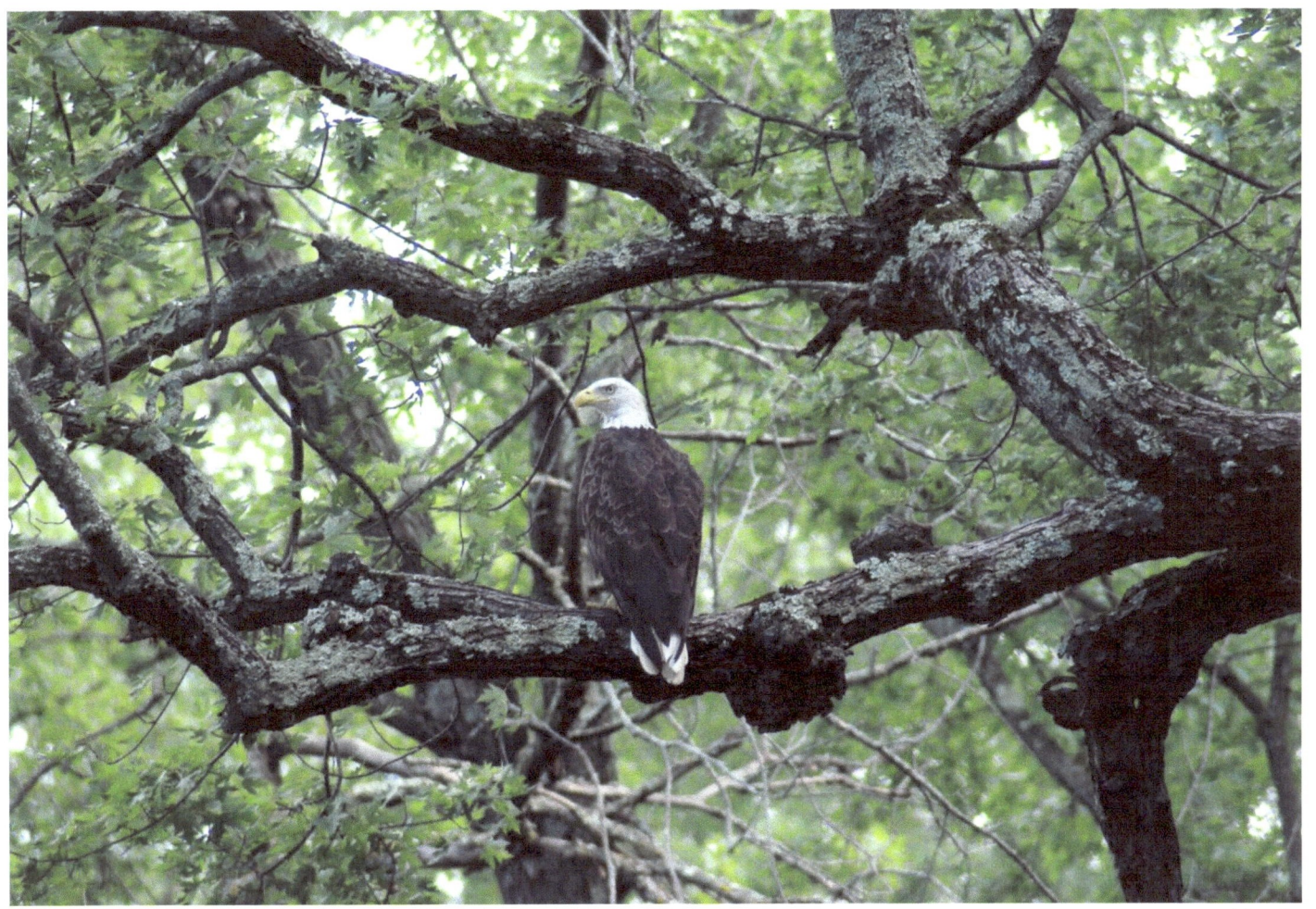

Bald Eagle

kayaking down a lazy river –
from moss covered branches
we are watched

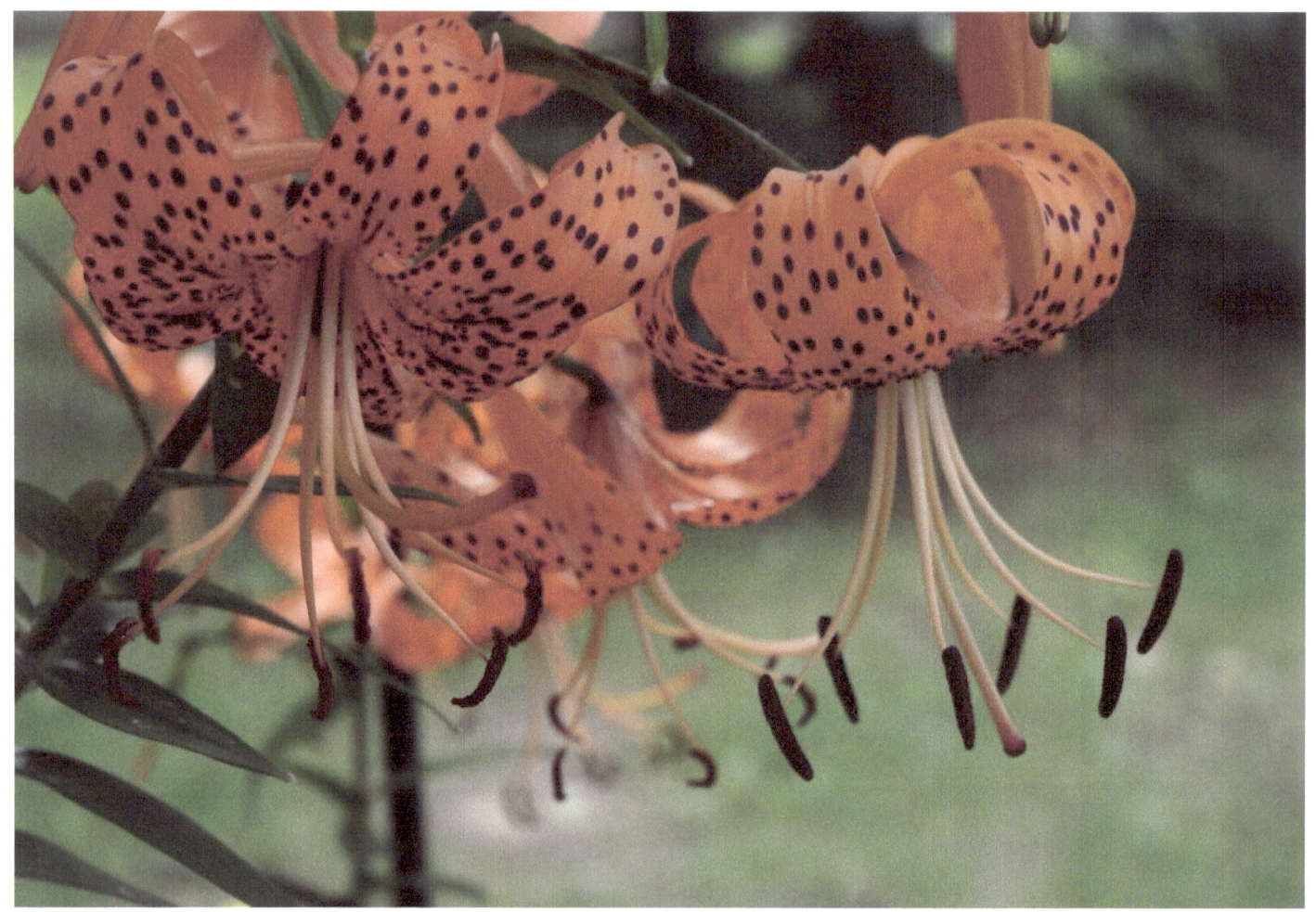

Tiger Lilies

ladies lift their skirts
showing their dancing feet

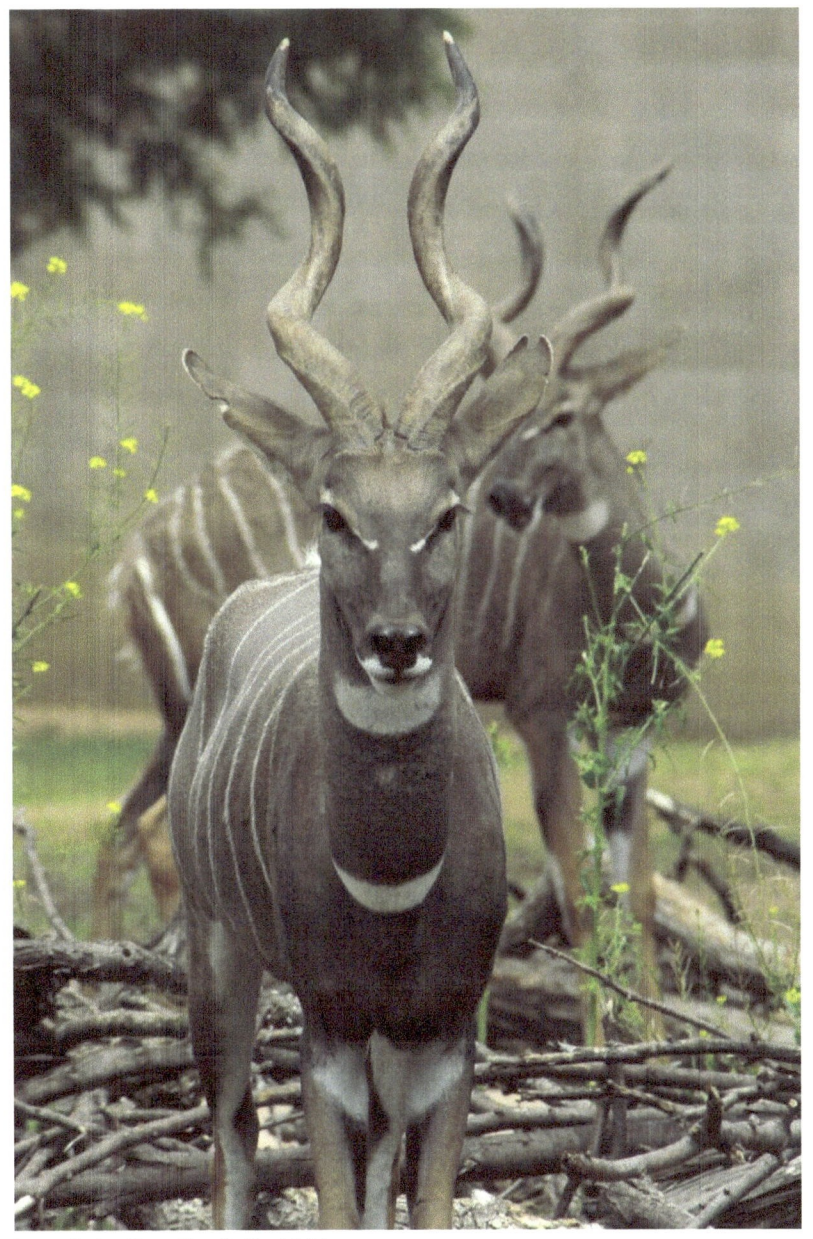

Lesser Kudu - Como Zoo, St. Paul, MN

attitude
in every line –
staring

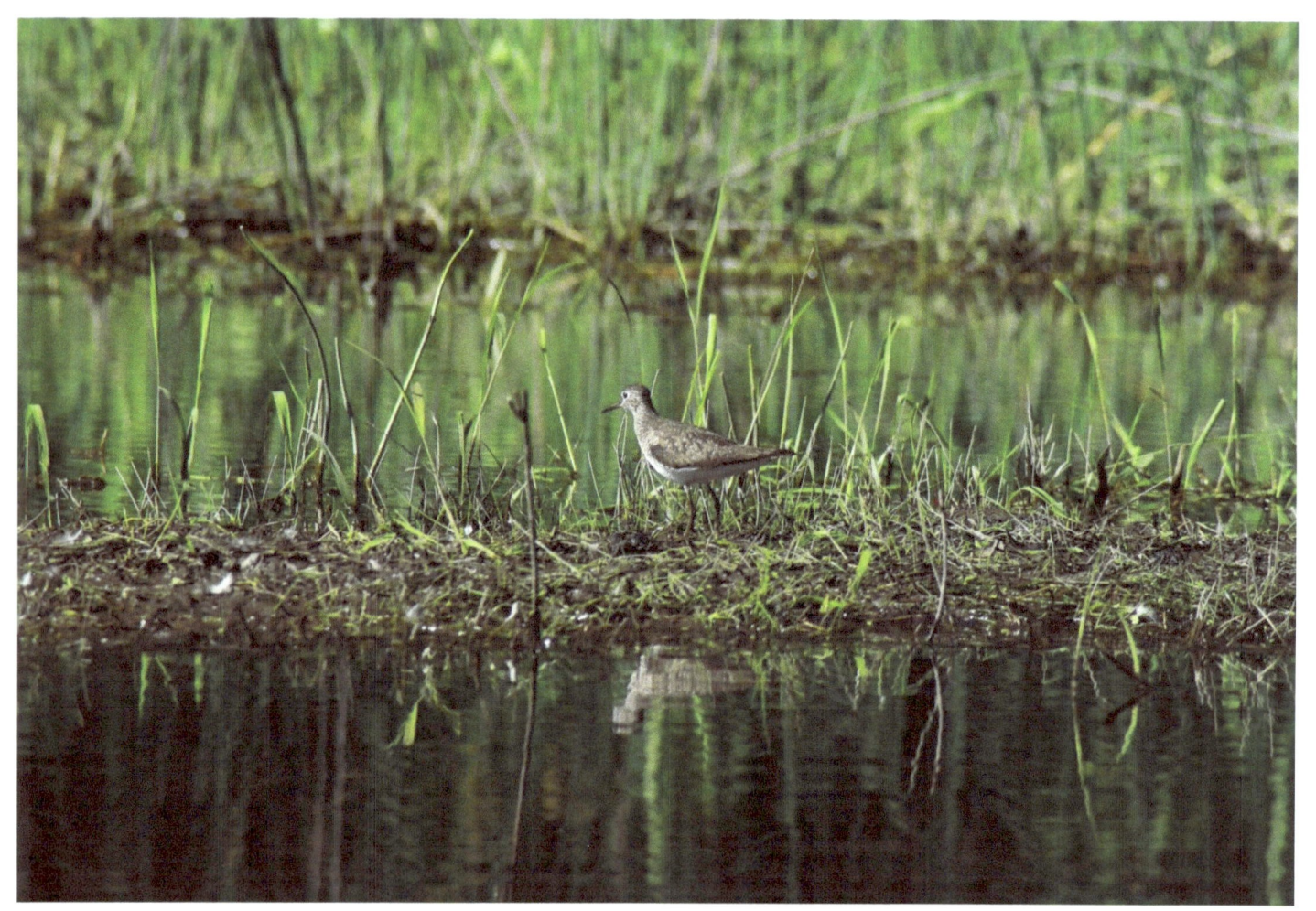

Solitary Sandpiper

Piper running
shadow keeping in stride -
lazy river

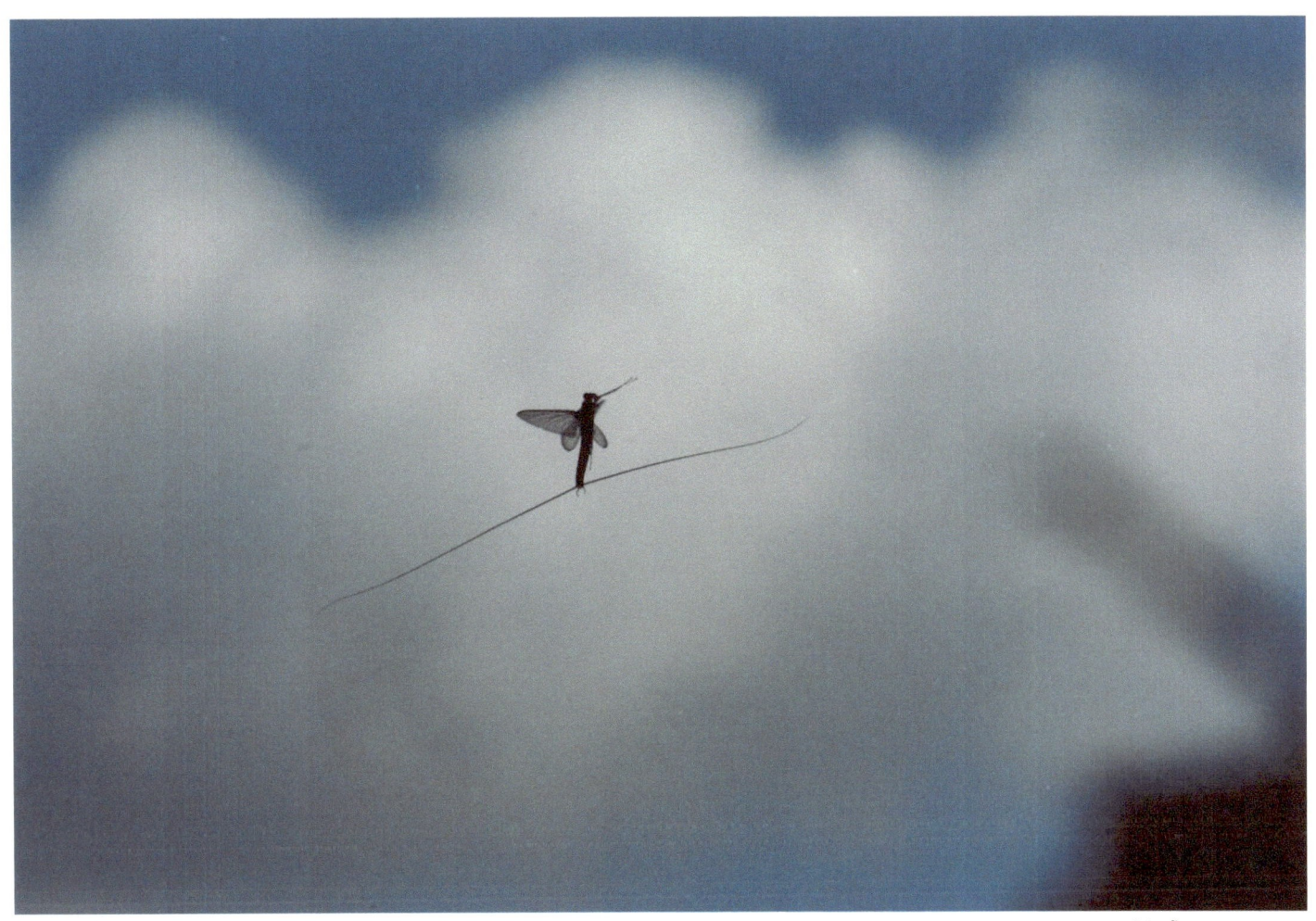

Mayfly

trapeze artist
on her own high wire

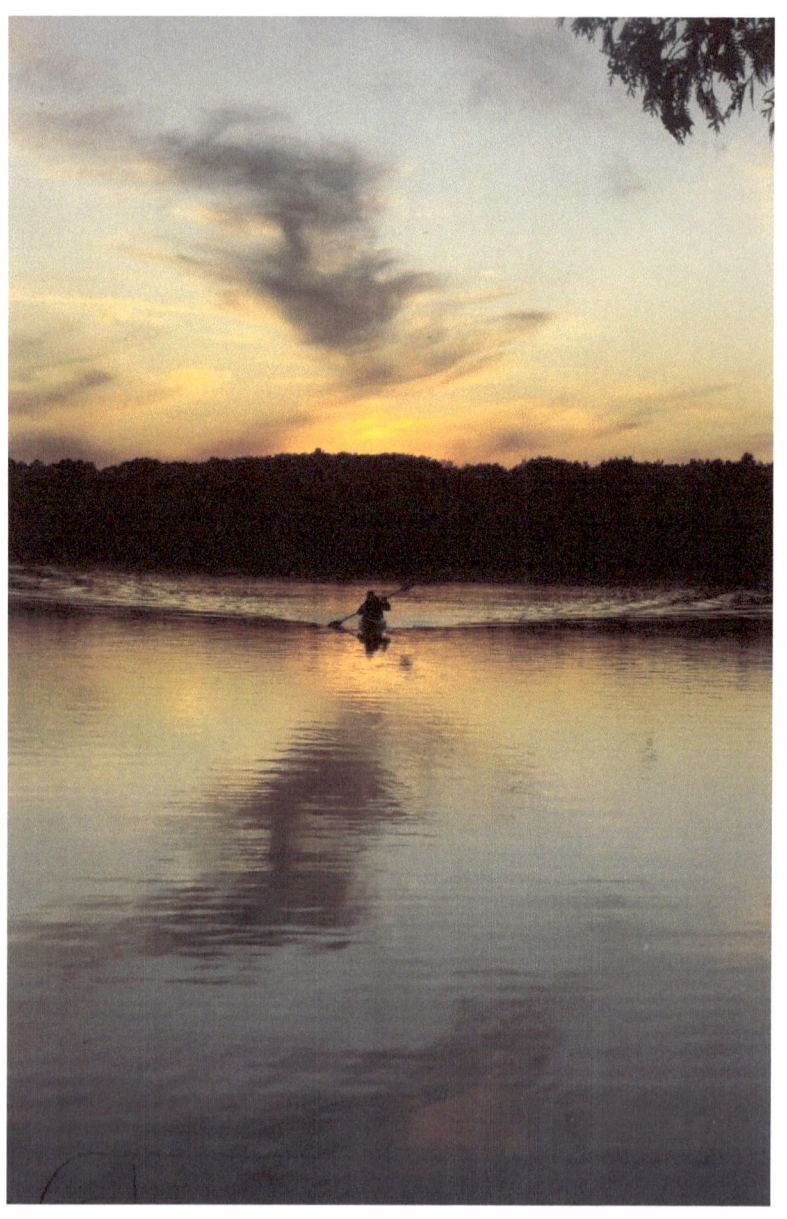

the kayaker
becomes one with the water –
evening sun

mountain moon
watching the sun
go to sleep

Autumn

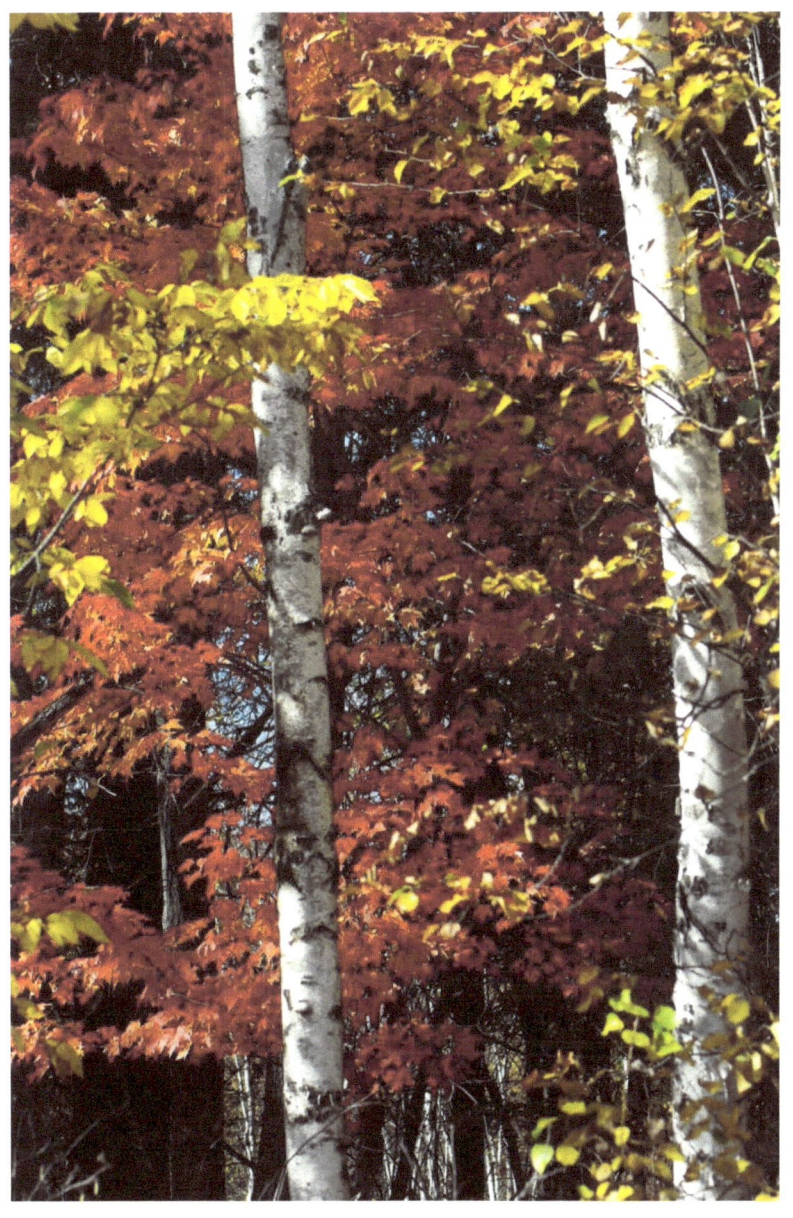

flame of autumn
inspires awe within my soul -
warmth

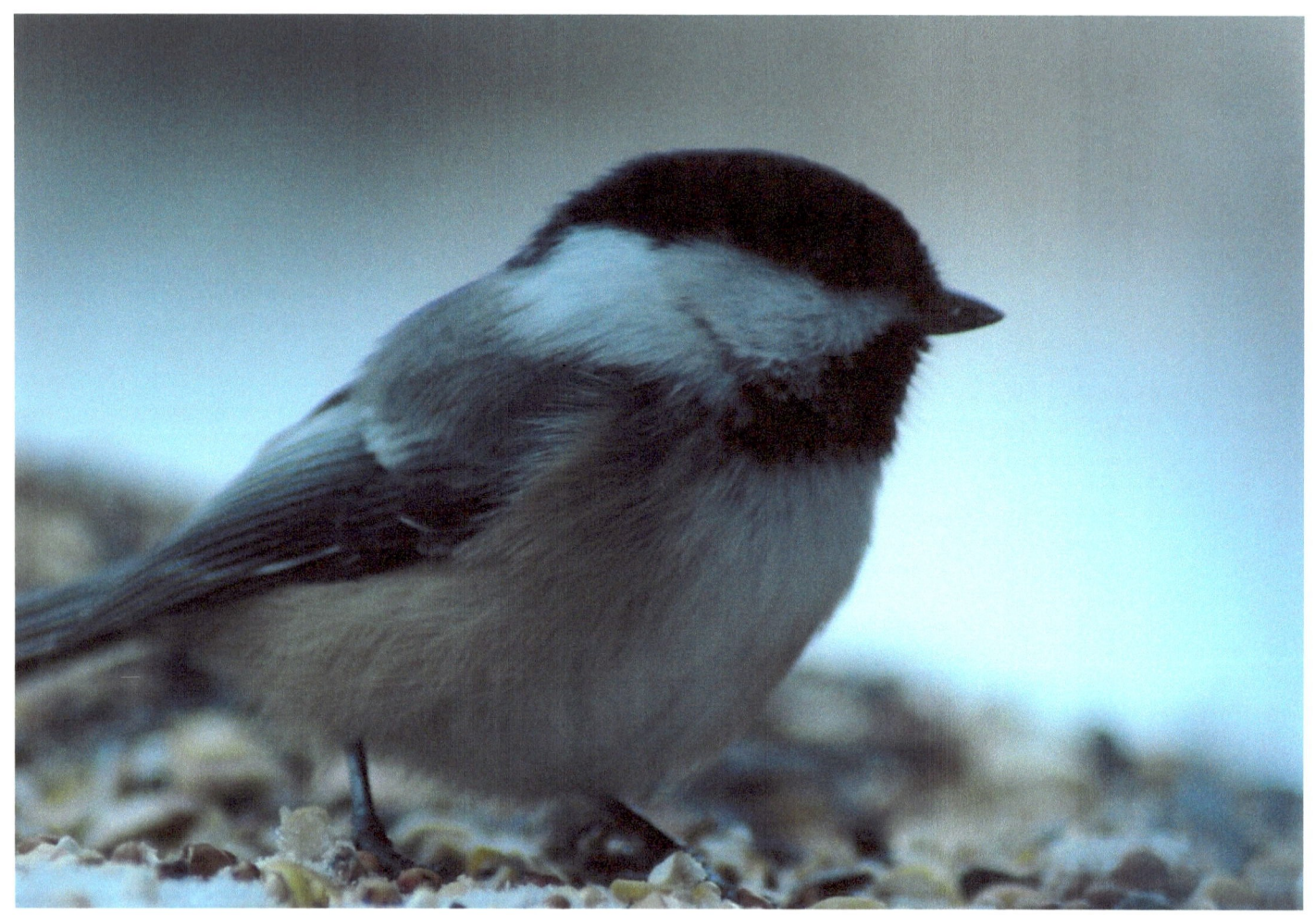

Black-capped Chickadee

ruffled feathers
by wind or stalking cat –
chickadee dinner

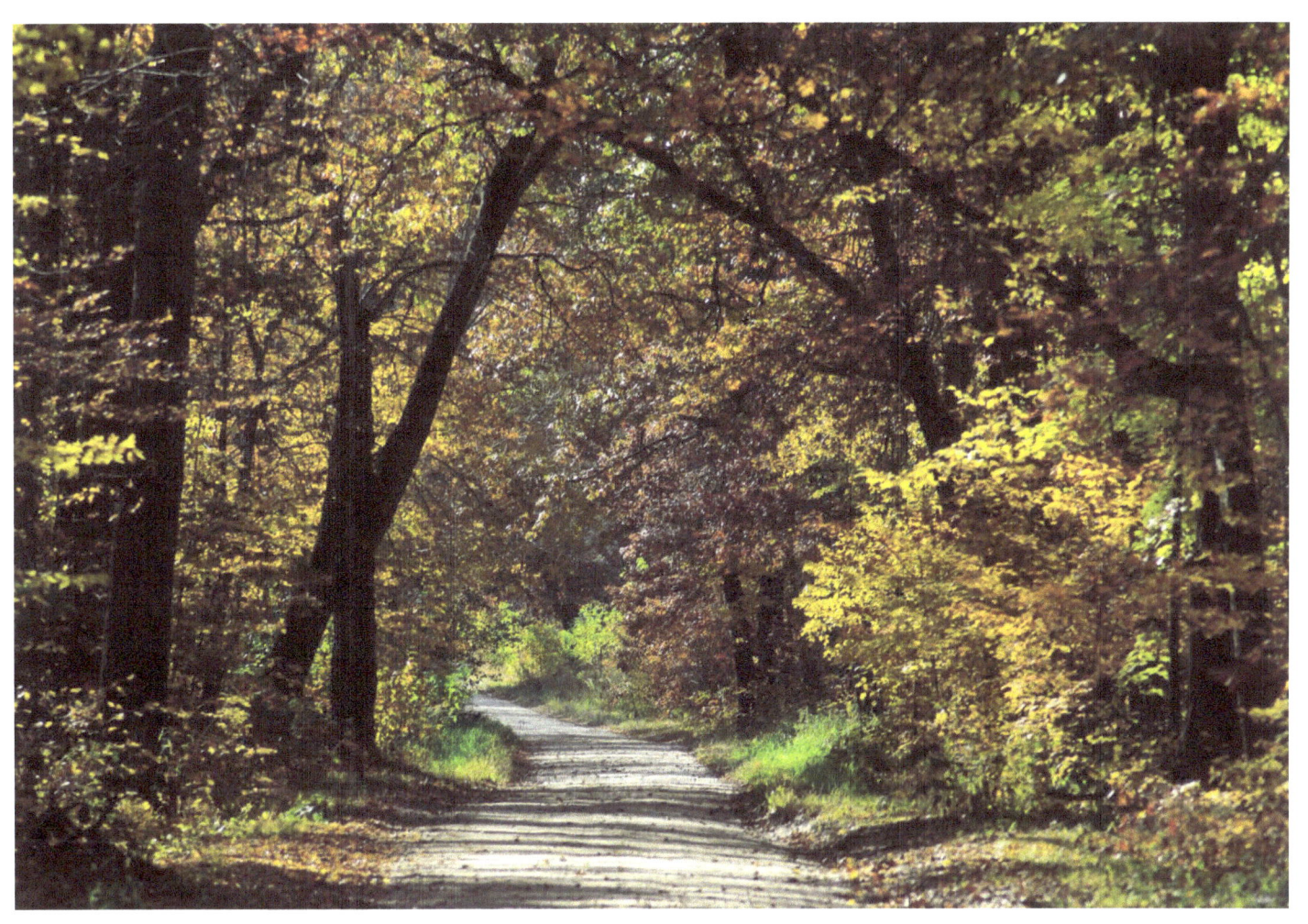

road of life
is not always paved -
golden opportunities within reach

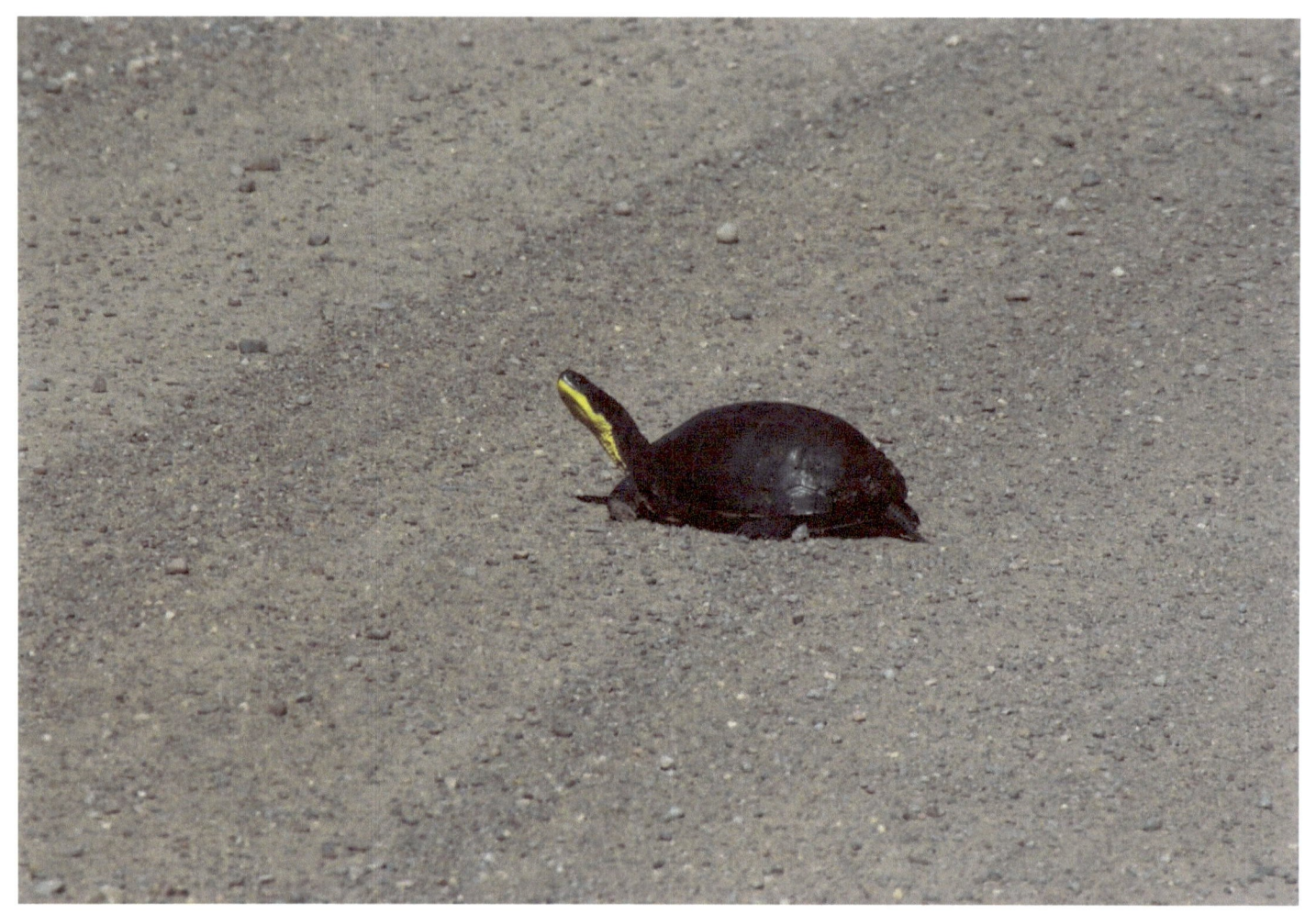

Blanding's Turtle

stopping
watching the turtle's journey
going no where

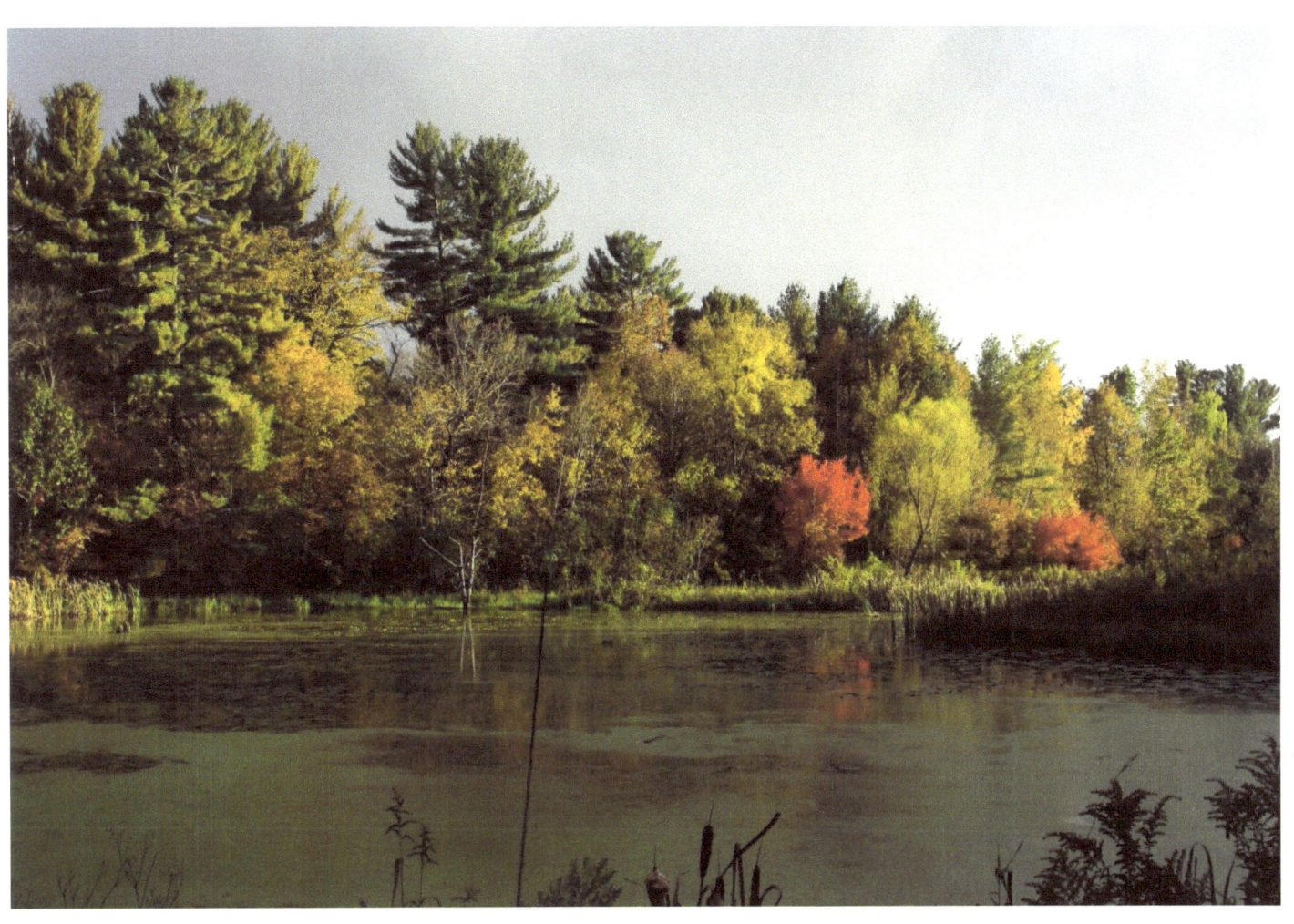

a beacon
beckons across the pond –
late autumn

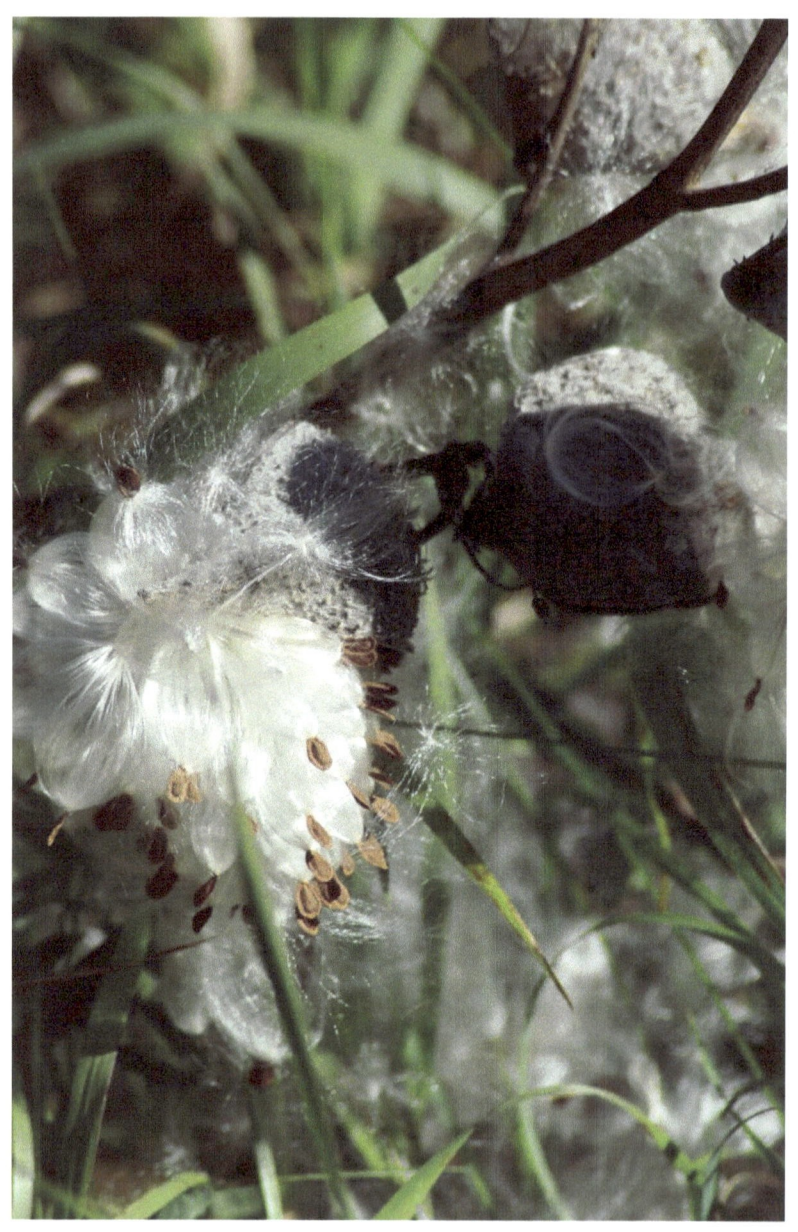

milkweed filaments
within my pillow –
insulation for my dreams

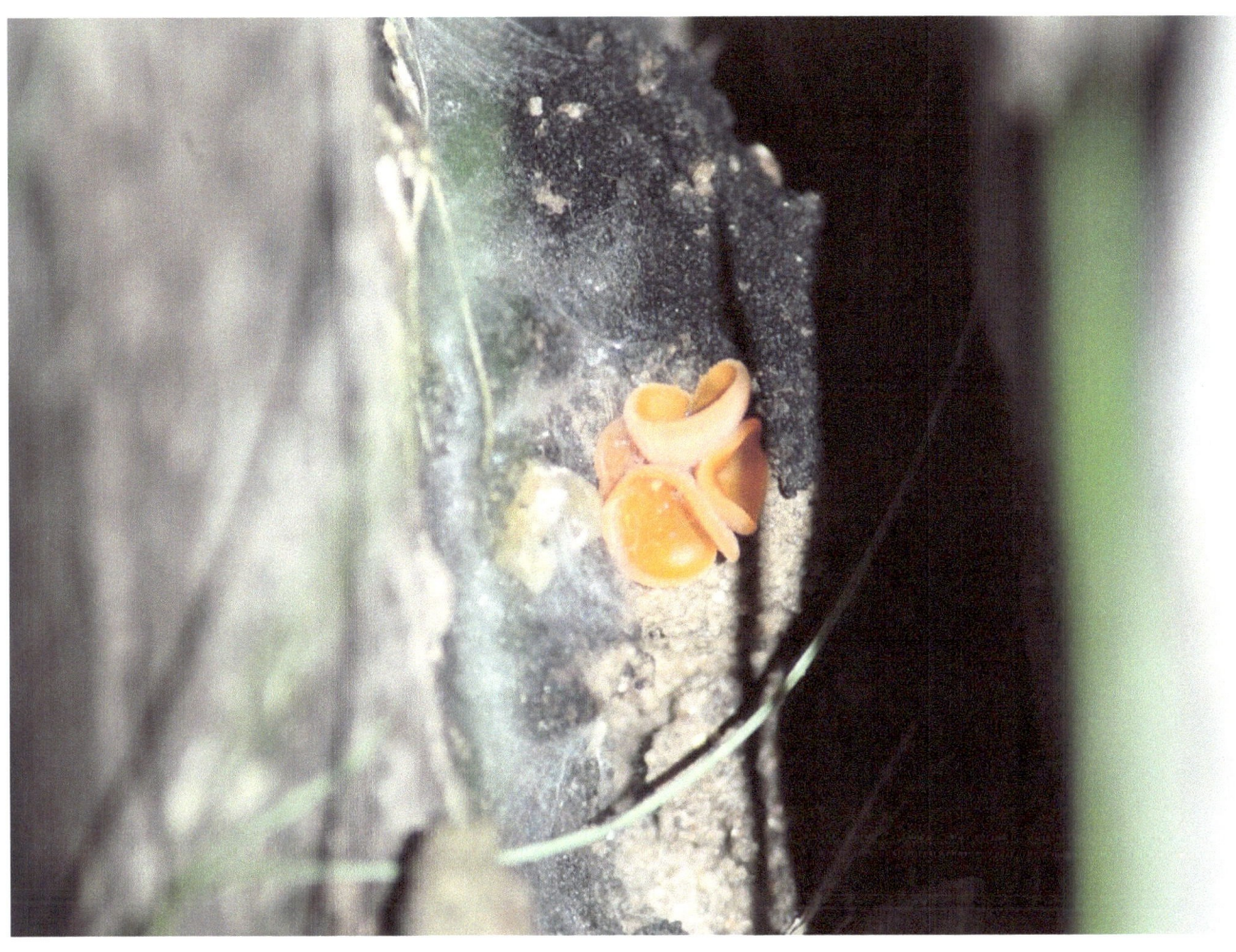

lucky glimpse
shows me the beauty
hidden within a crevice

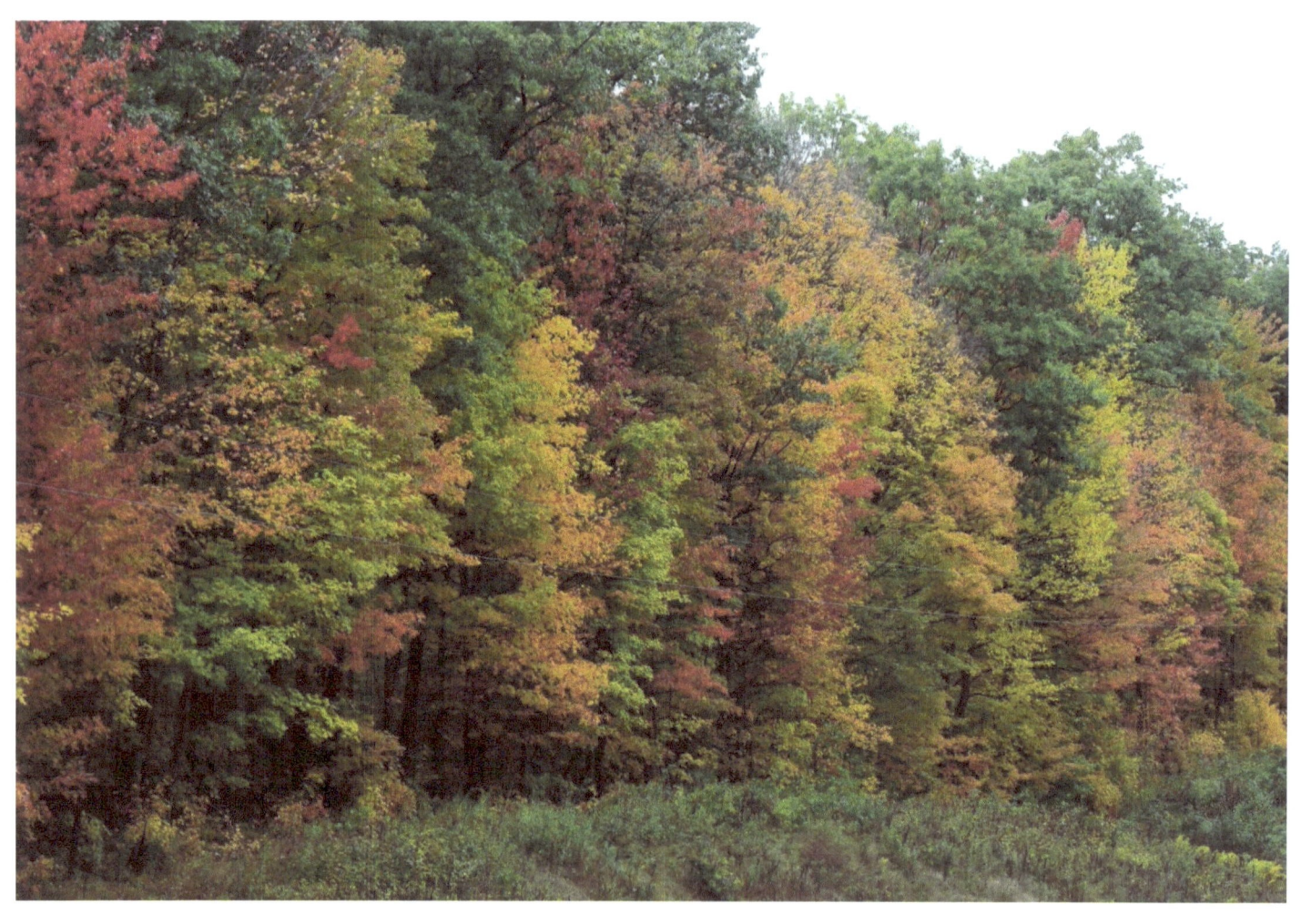

painter's palette
stretches along the road
brightening my journey

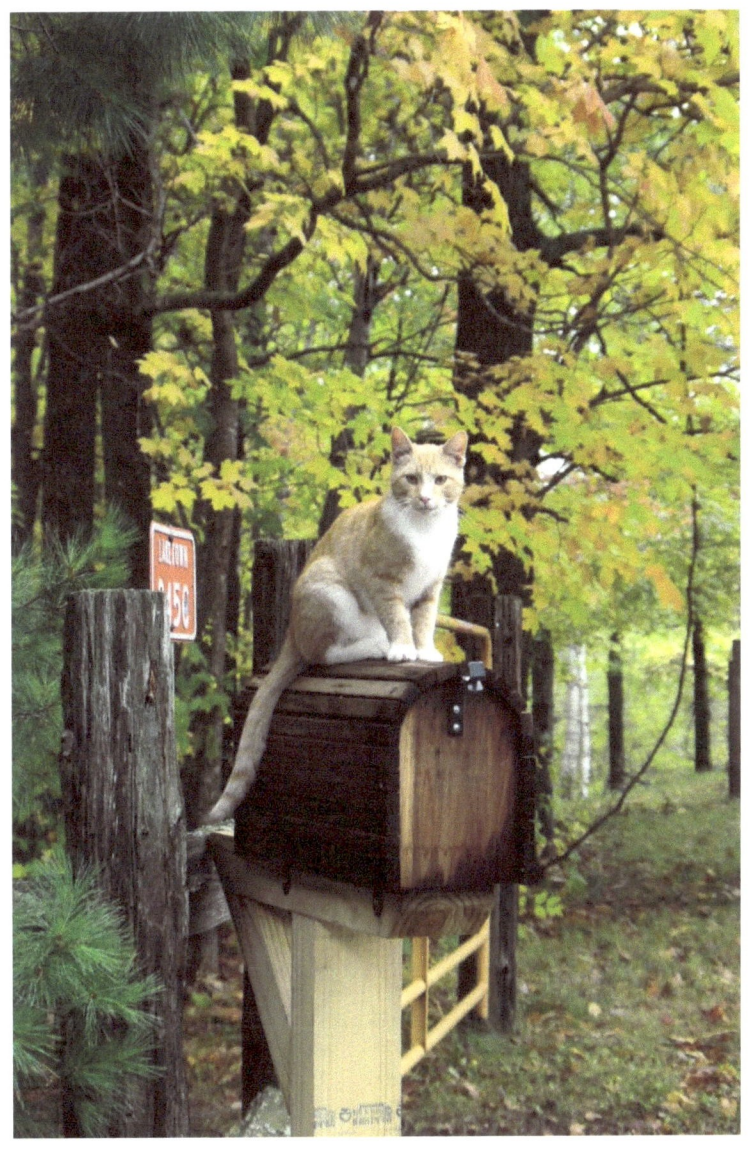

male
awaiting human correspondence
mailbox

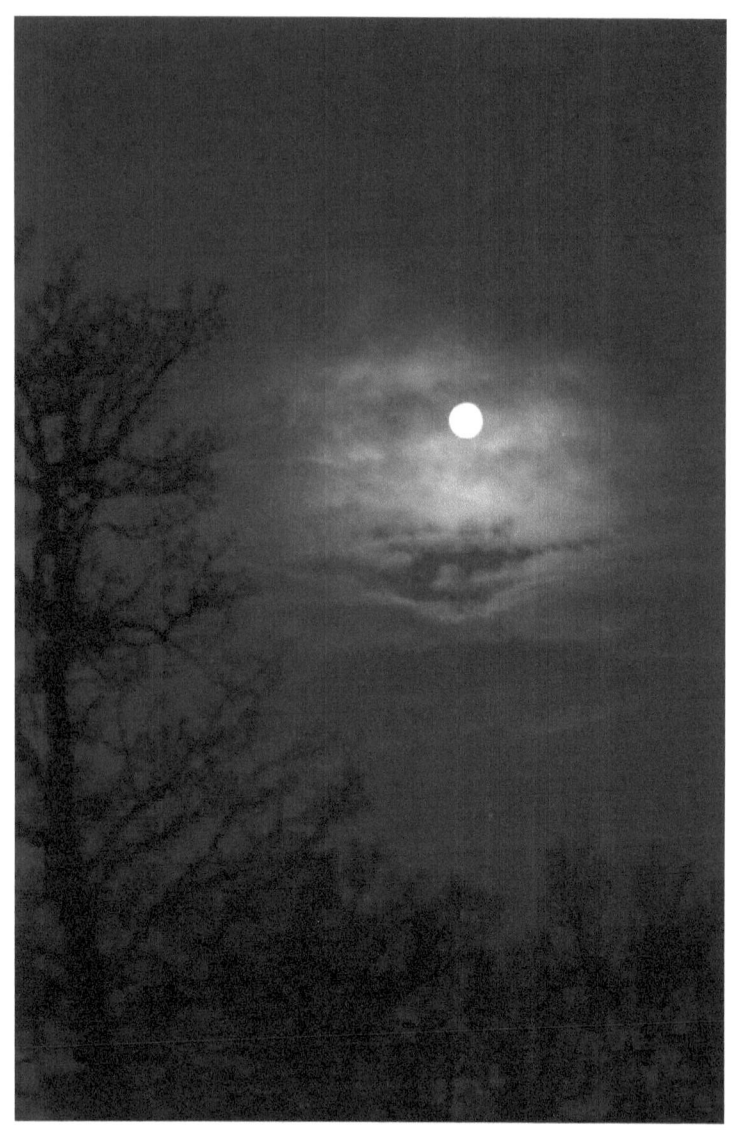

naked branches
silhouetted by evening's light
reaching, grasping – chilled

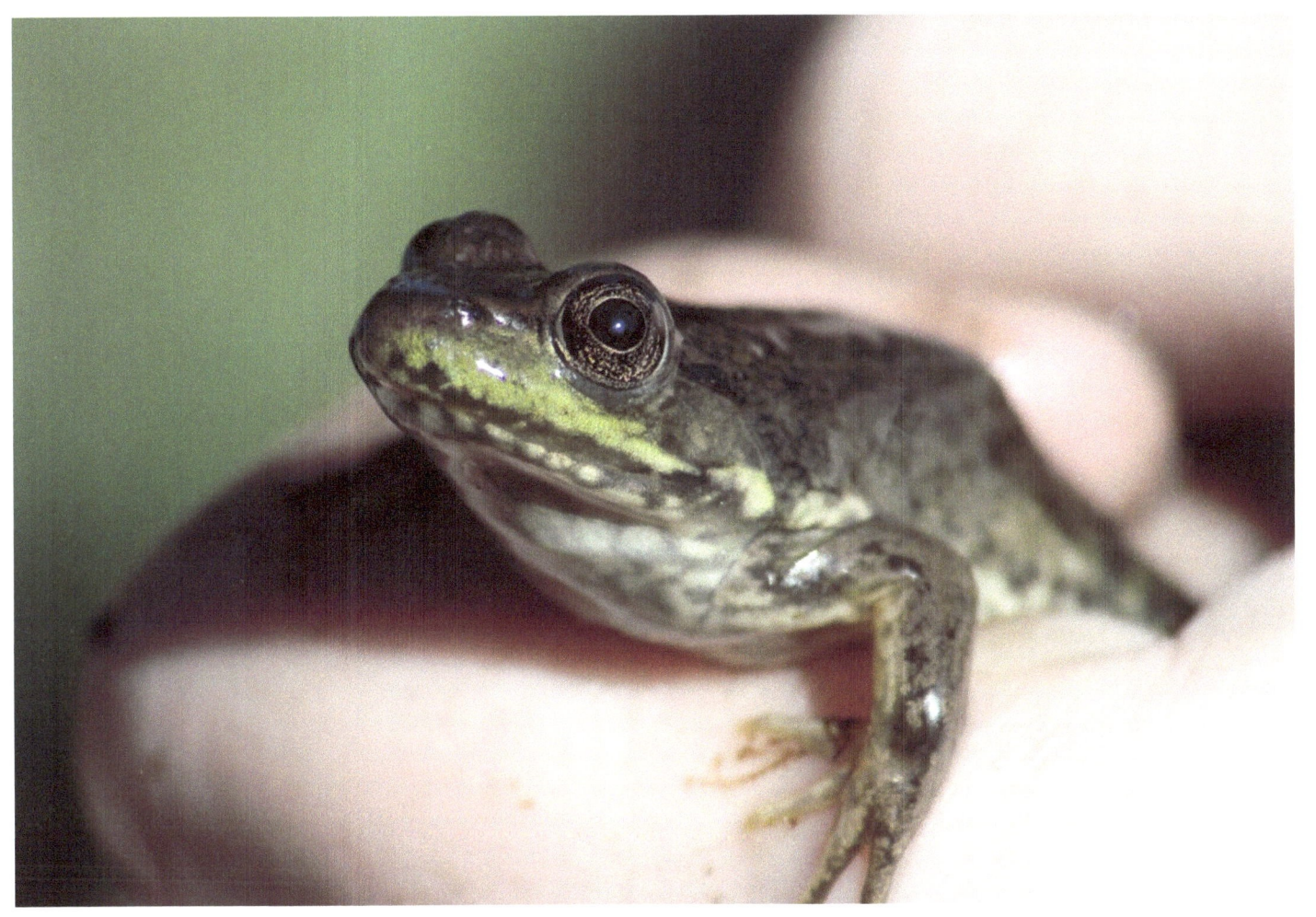

cold and wet
large eyes looking at me –
treasure in her hands

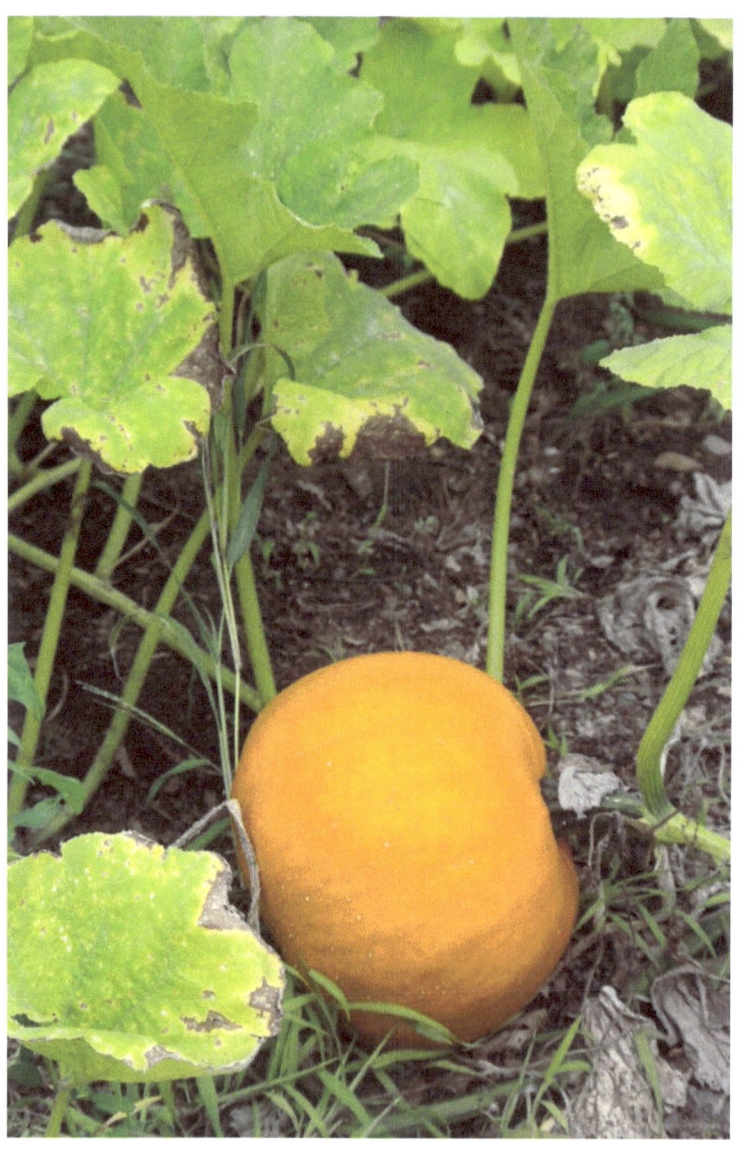

pumpkin, pumpkin on the vine
I shall pick you
then you will be mine

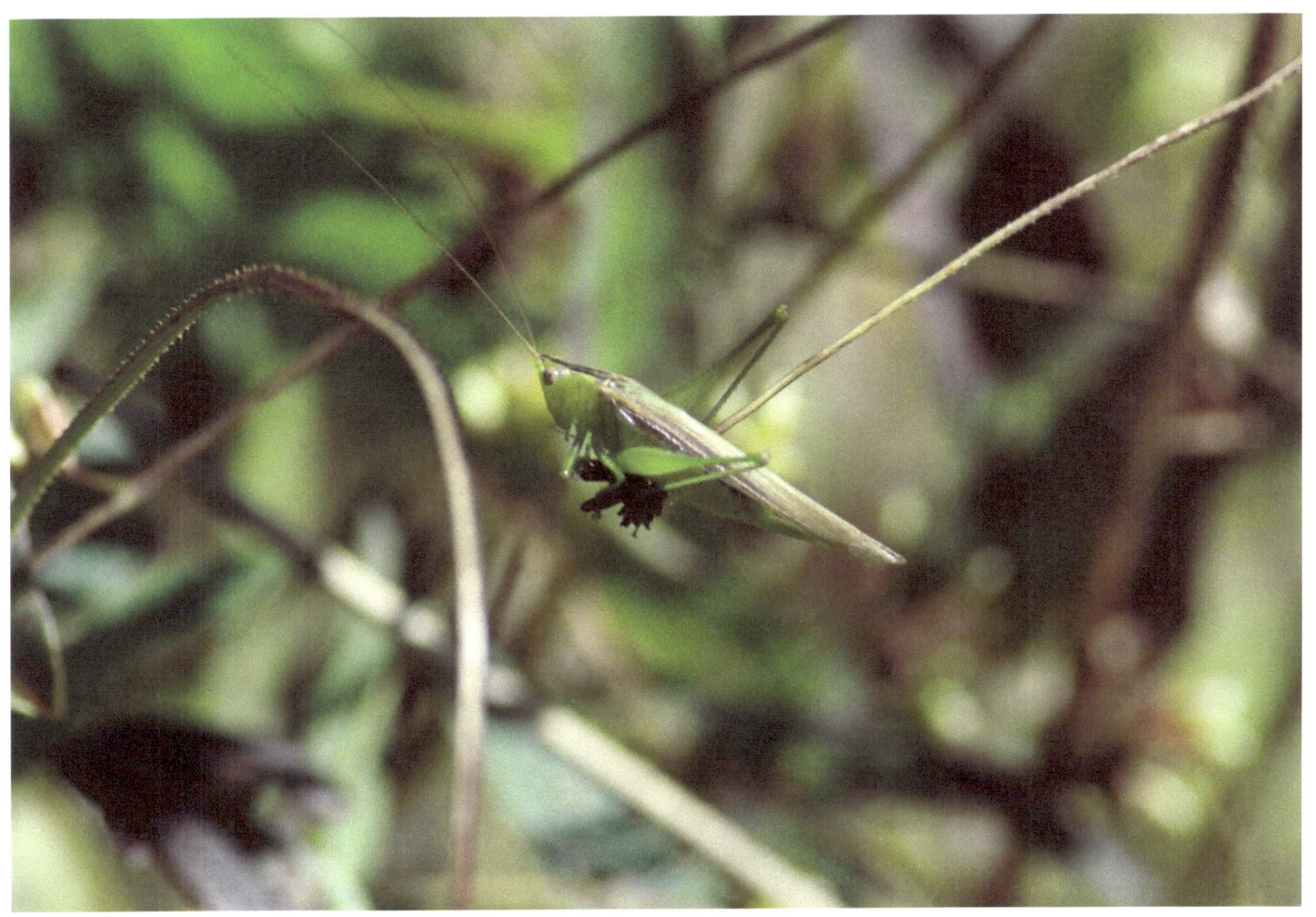

body translucent green
wings of straw upon your back -
hidden

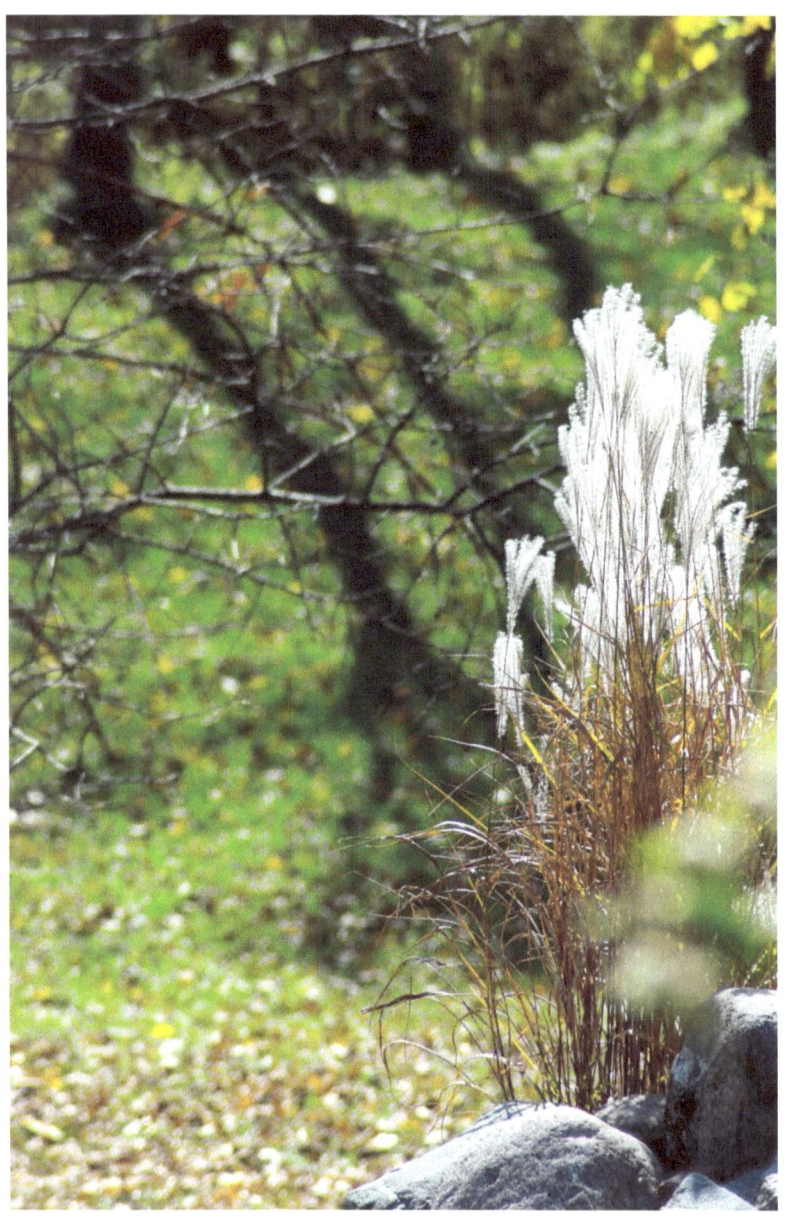

shining like an
upside down chandelier –
feathers of long prairie grass

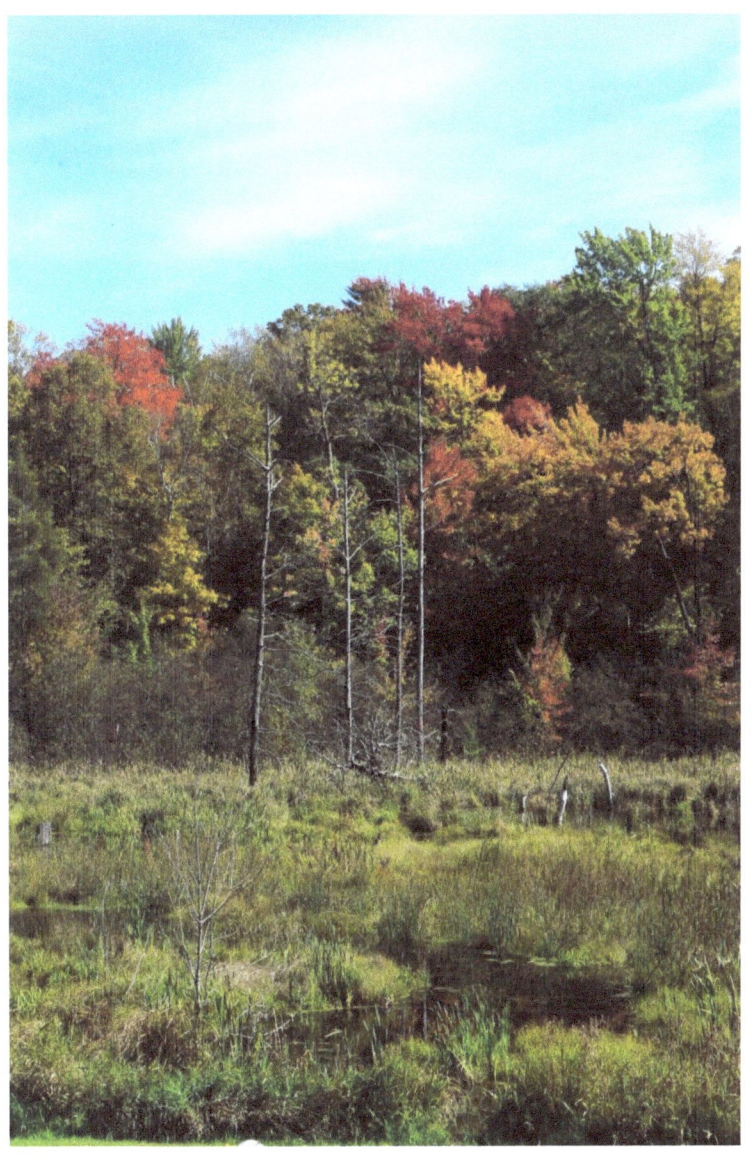

silent sentinels in a drying swamp
surrounded by a color guard

Winter

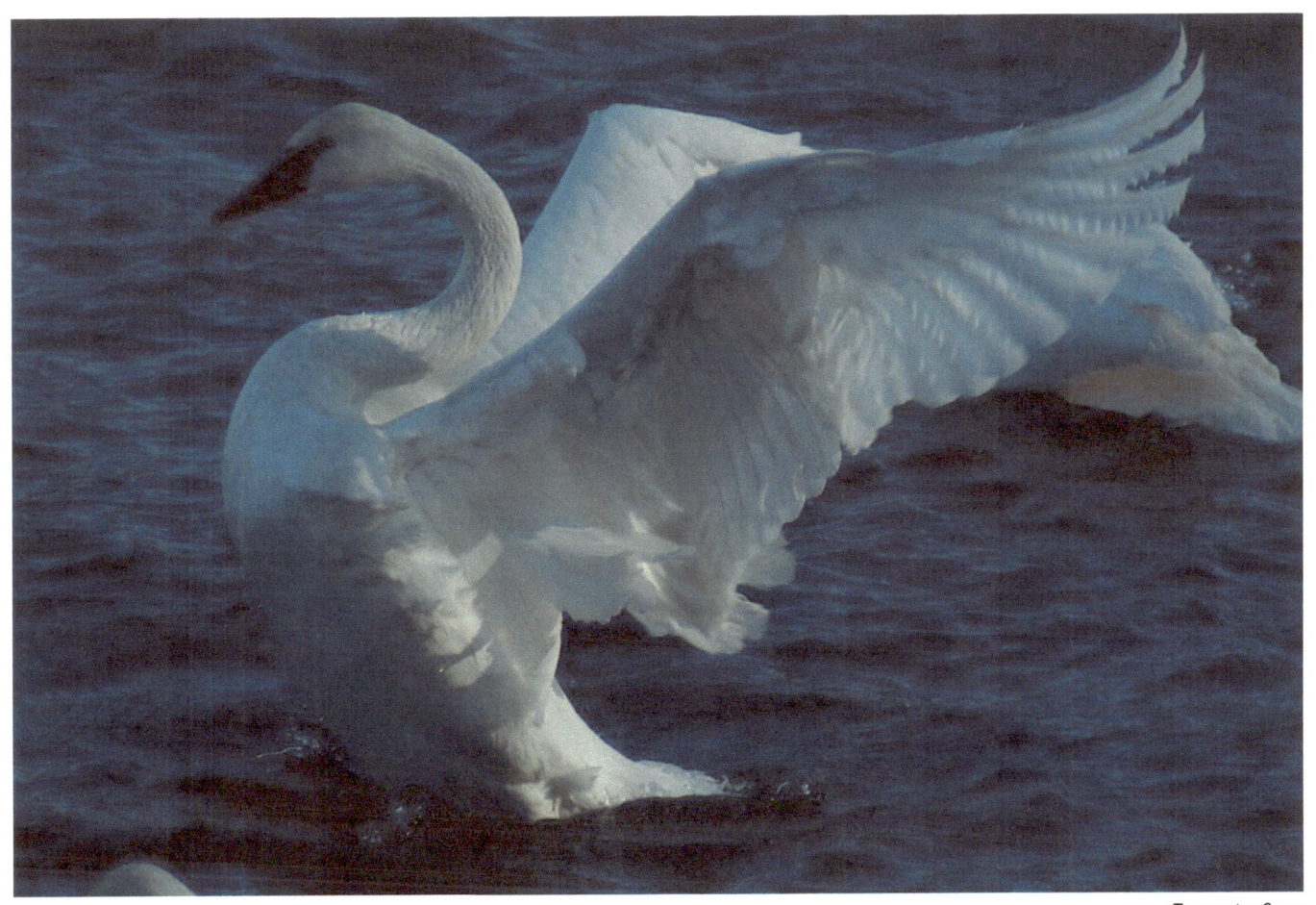

Trumpeter Swan

no other of God's creature's
can make me gasp with awe
as earth's angel

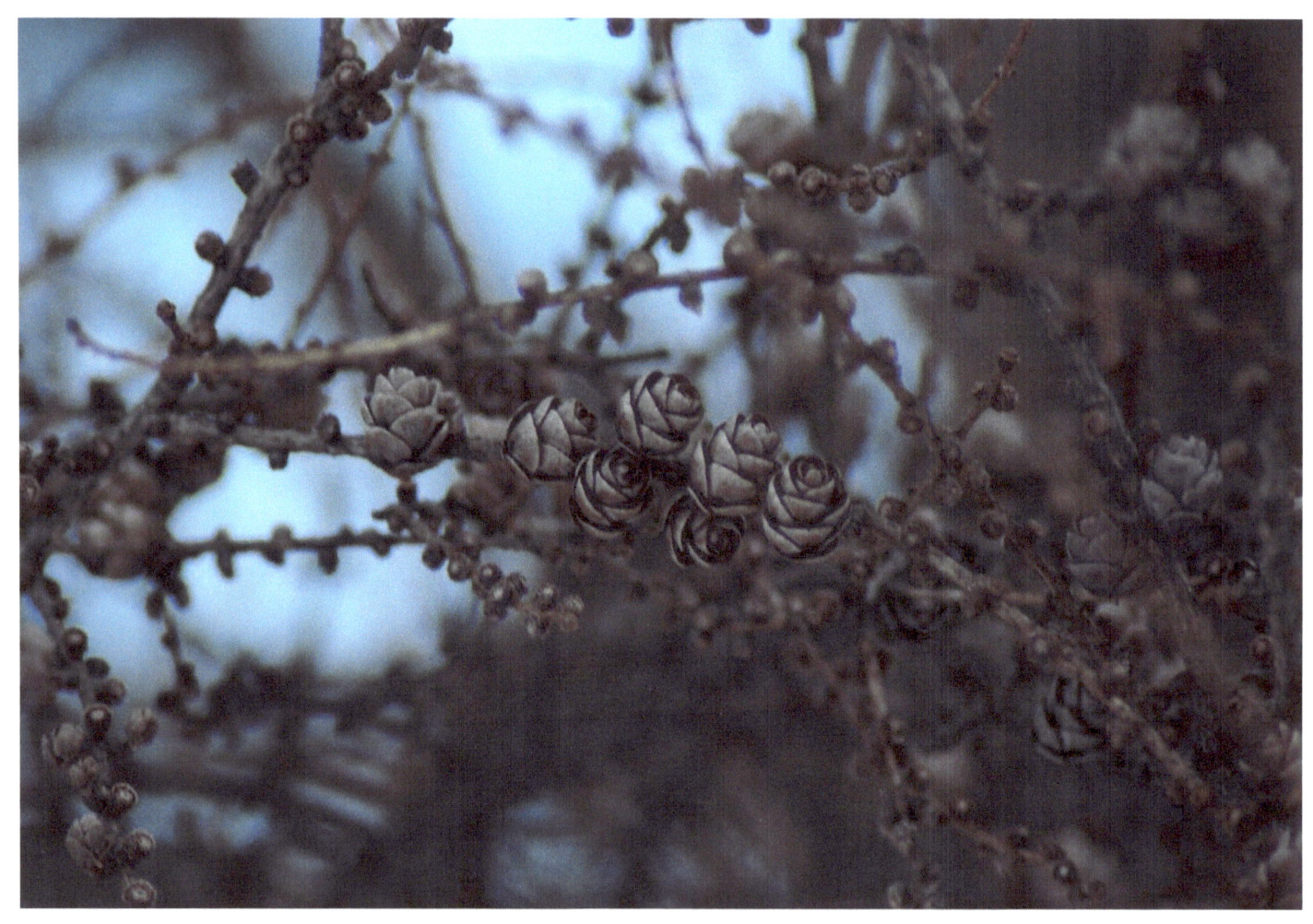

Tamarack
with your needles bare
so many pine cones
no wonder you have no hair!

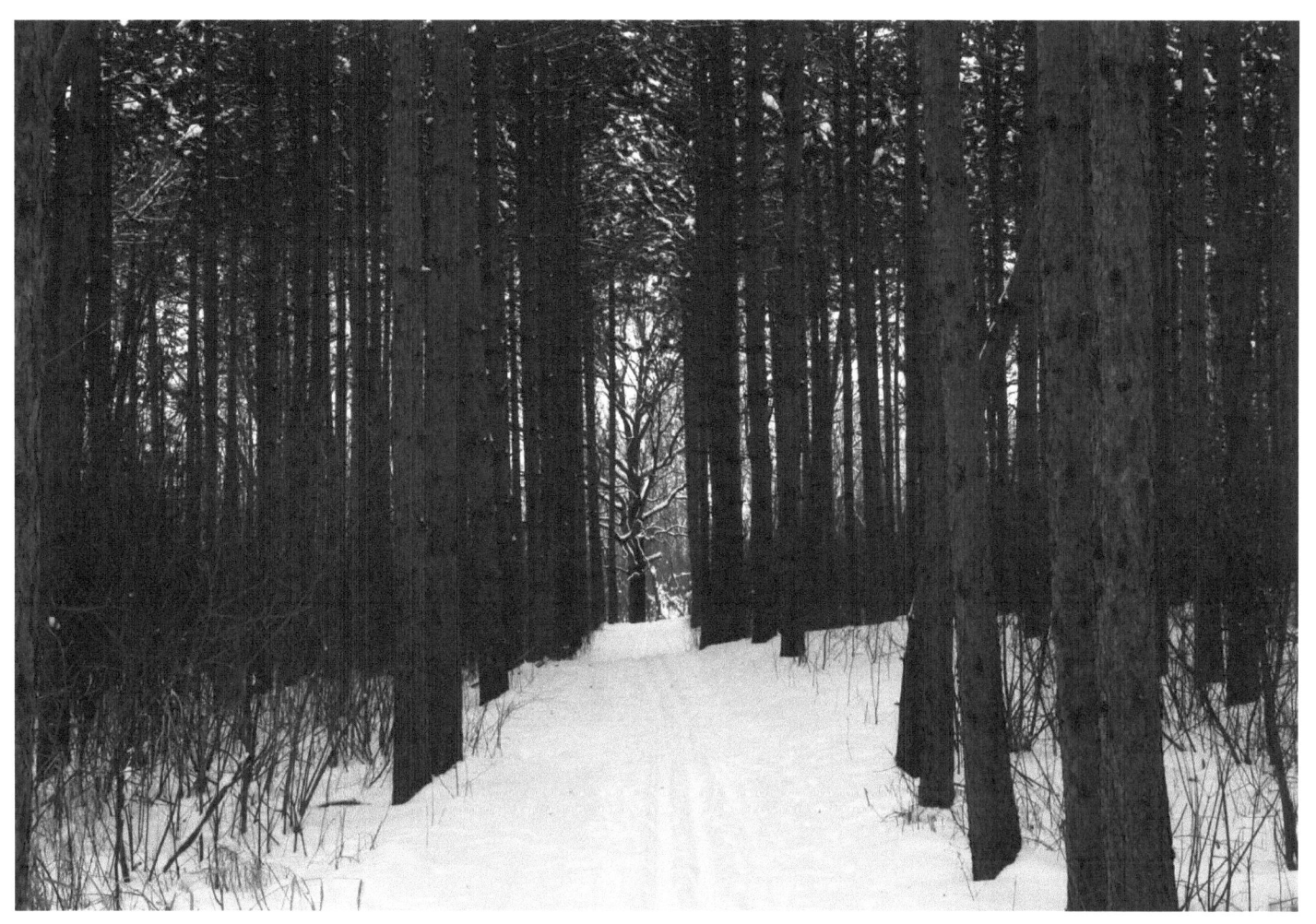

a row of courtiers
grace the path between
me and the gnarled, old king

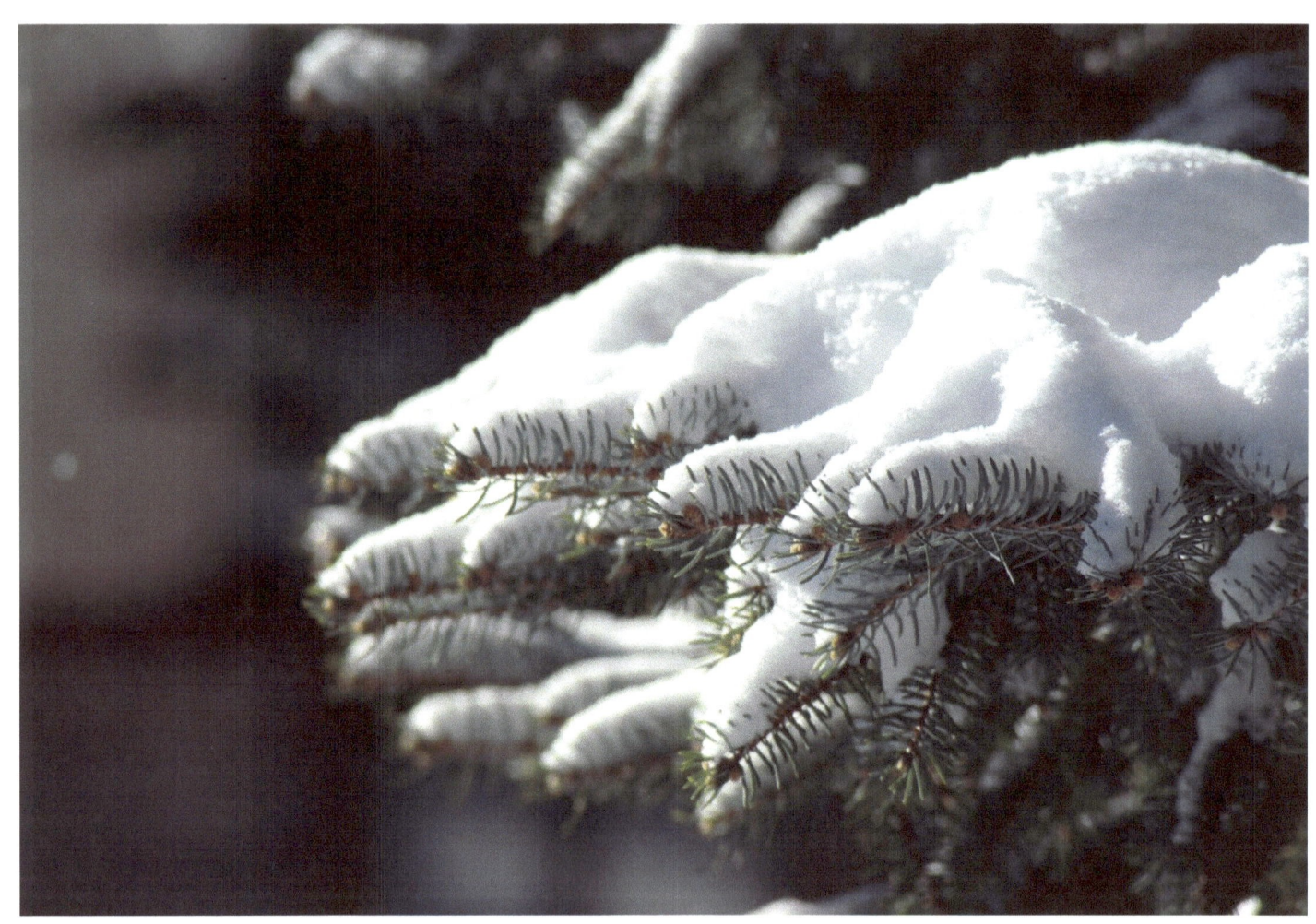

whimsical mountains
upon the pine boughs –
fairies ski here

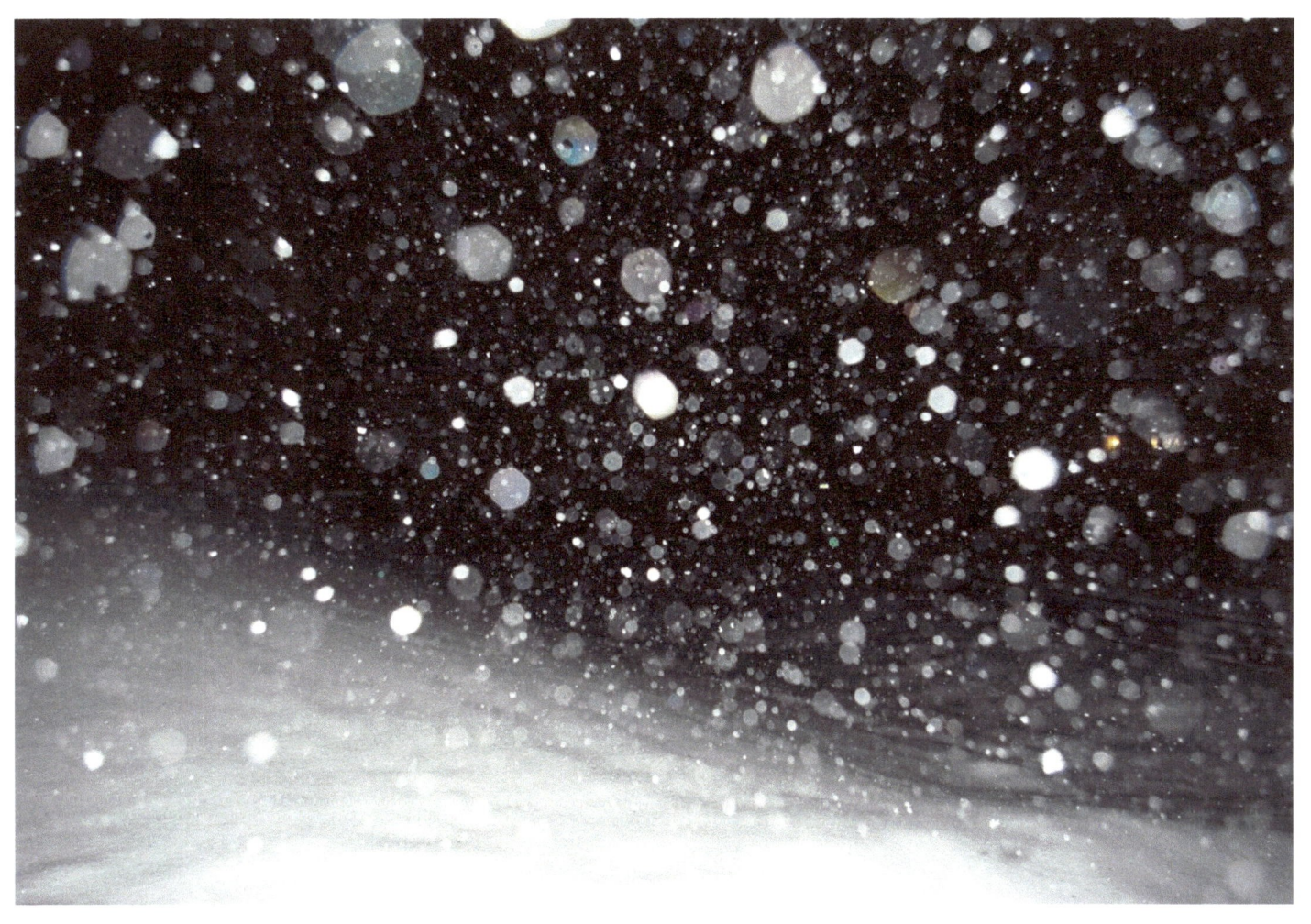

Blizzard –
Fibonacci flakes
captured in the light

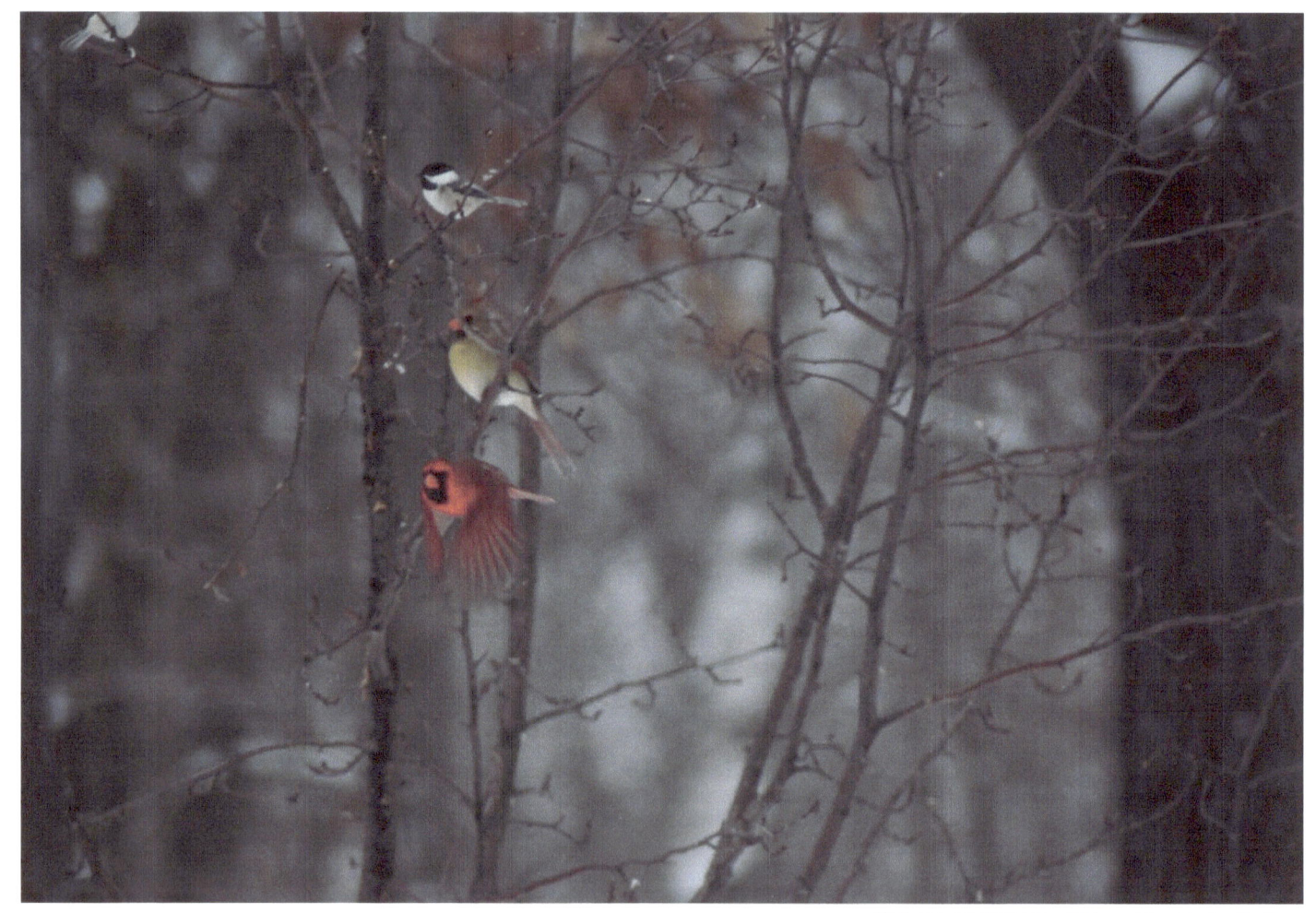

Black-capped Chickadee, Male and Female Cardinals

queuing up for dinner -
next

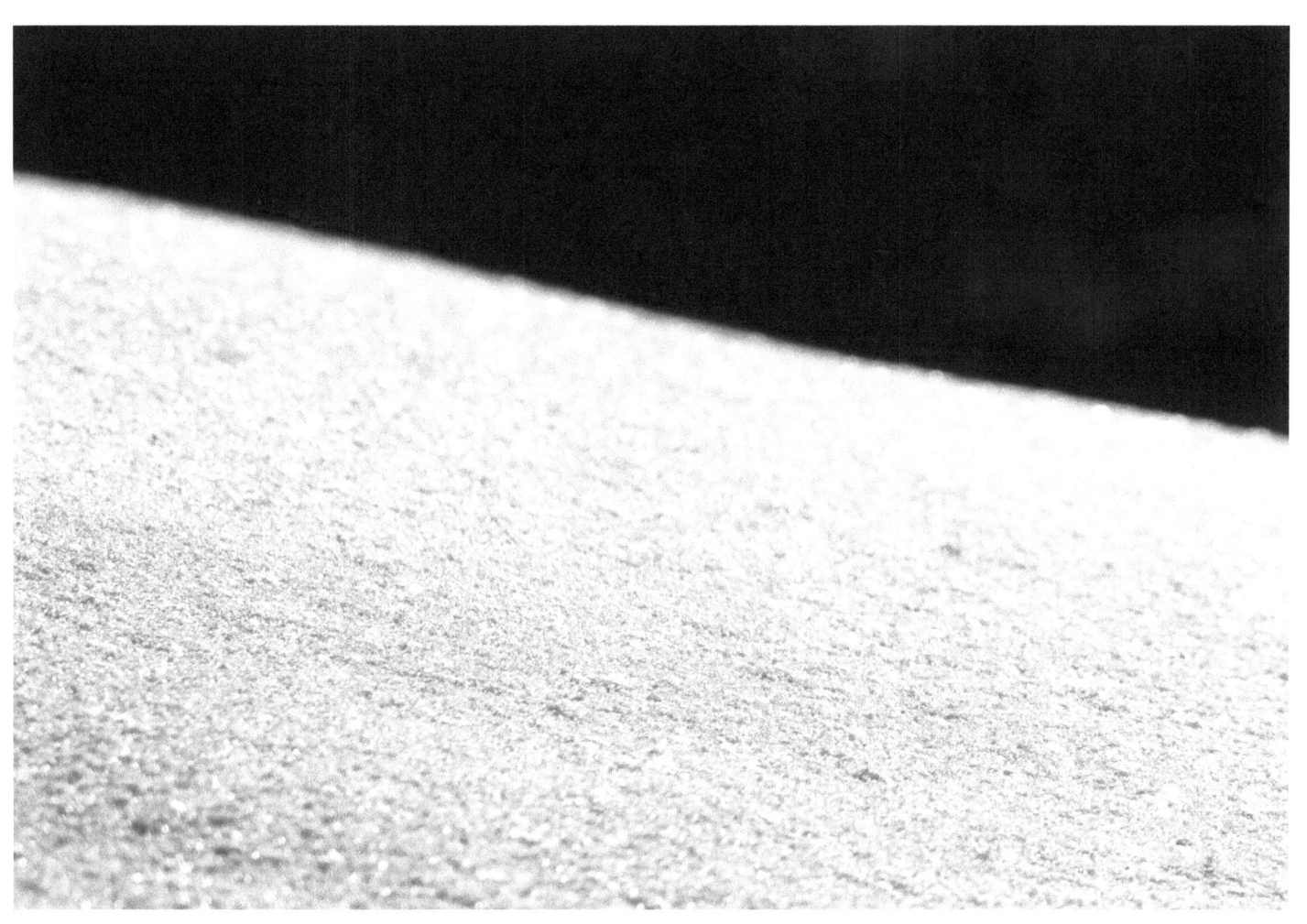

Snow –
Winter's diamonds upon the ground

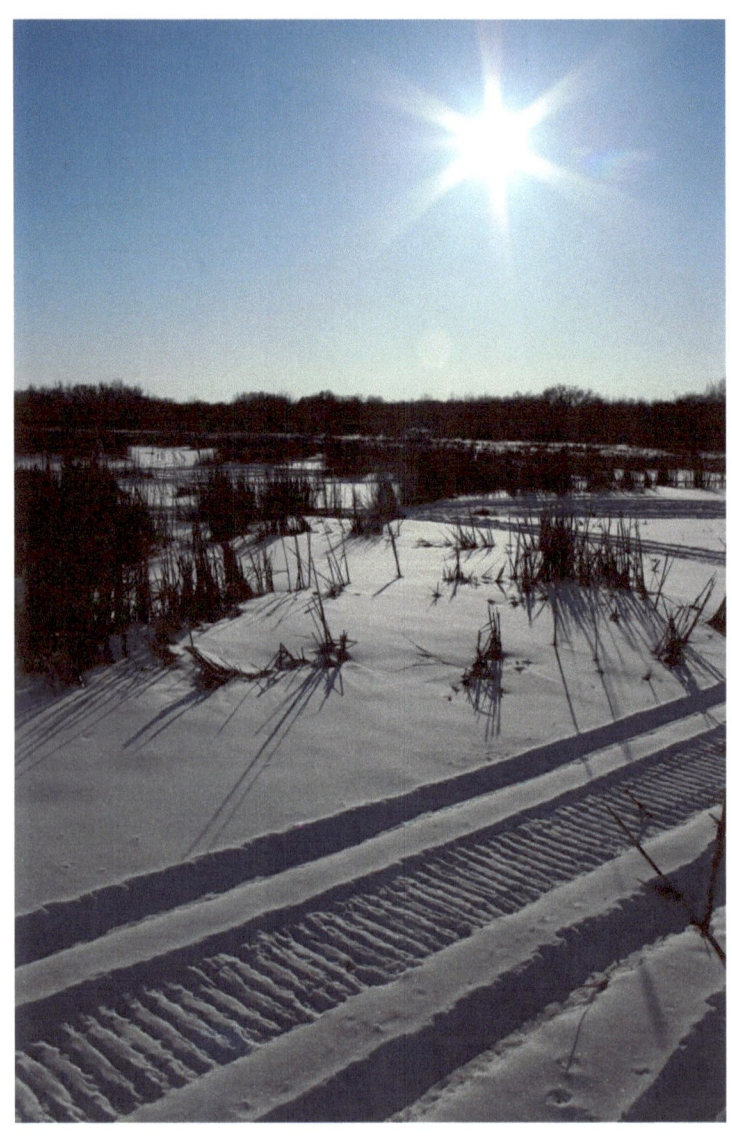

daylight's star
barely warms my skin
as shadows grow

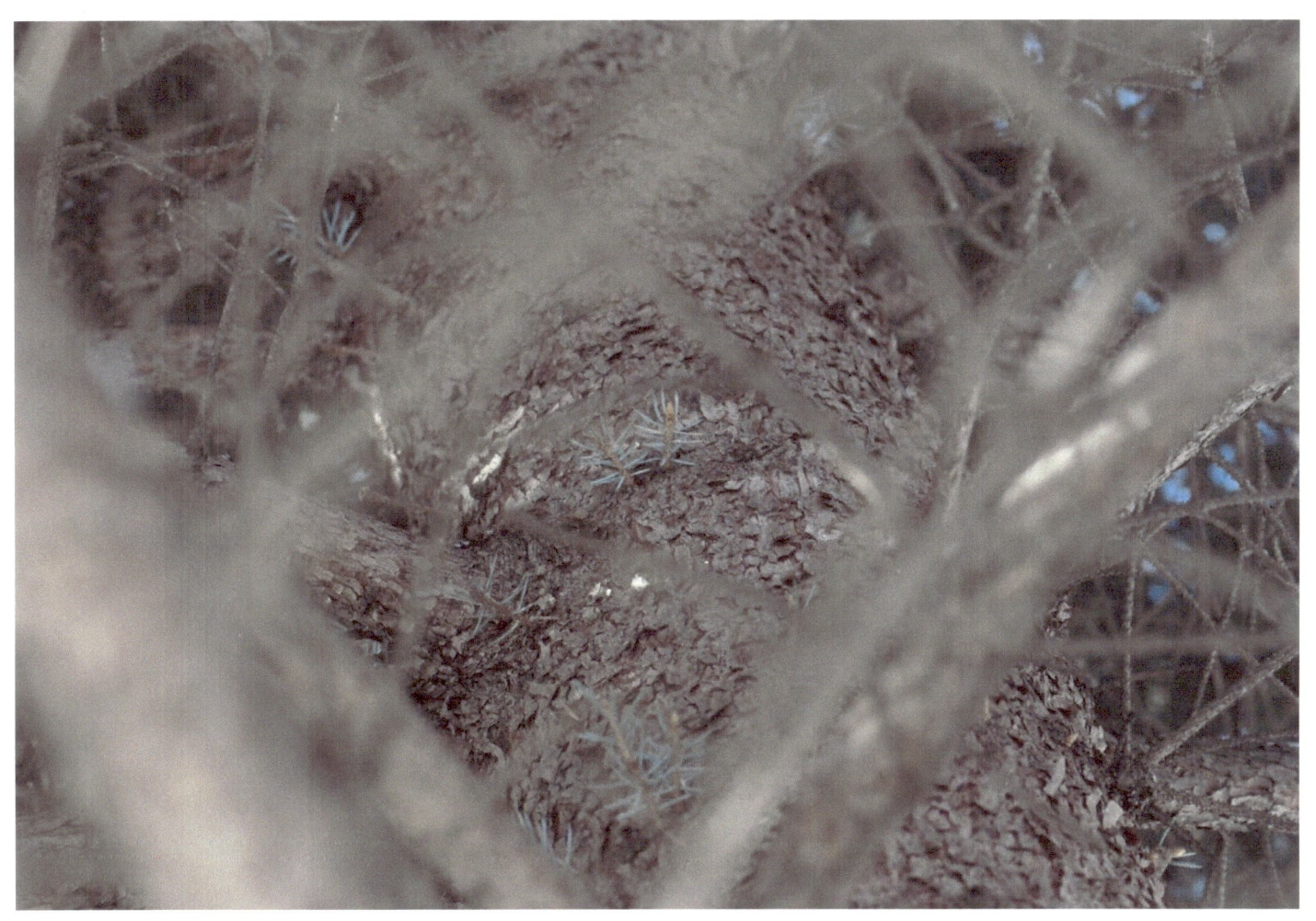

betwixt the branches
of the everlasting Spruce –
new growth

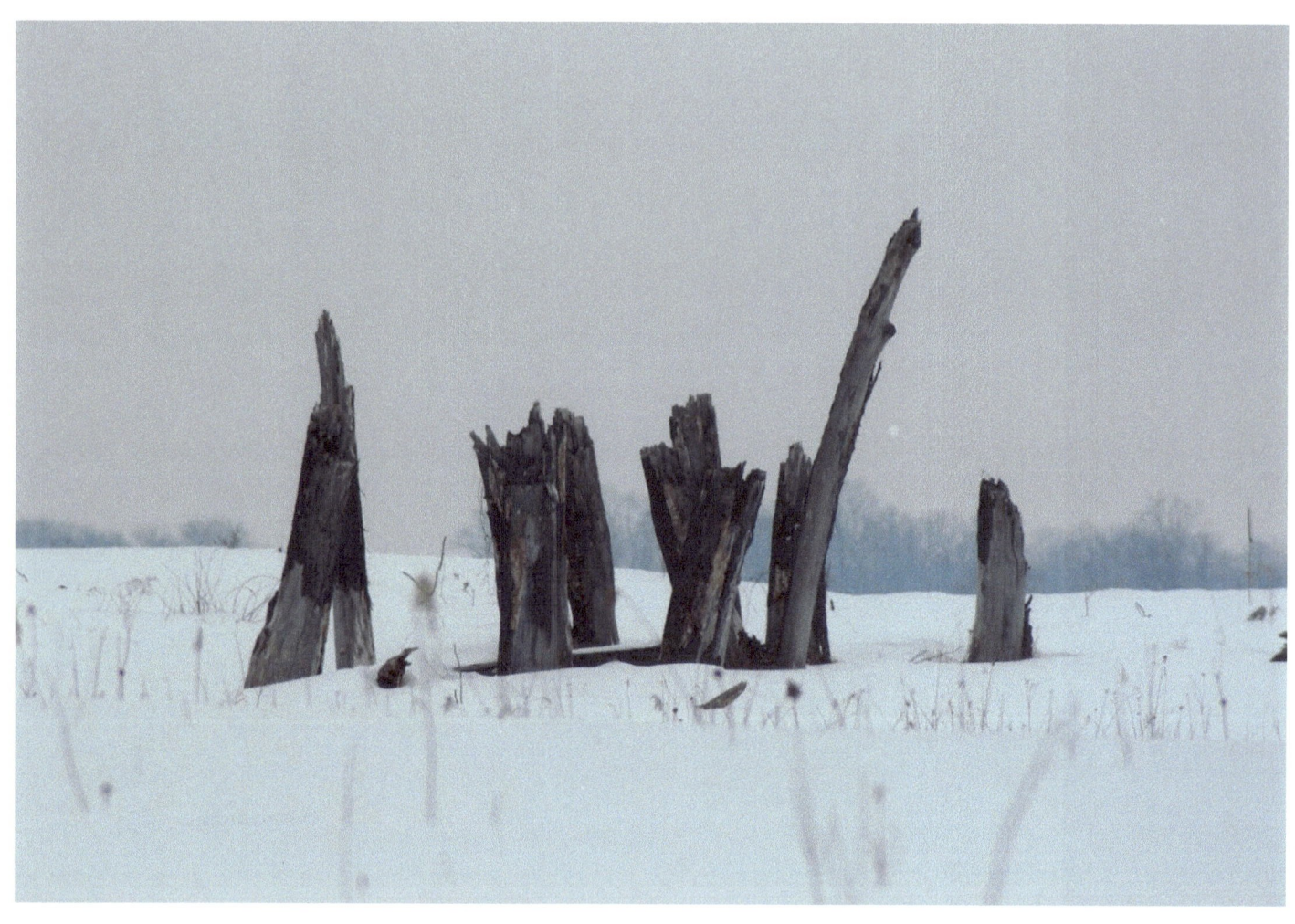

wooden circle
air crackles with mystical weight -
visions of Stonehenge

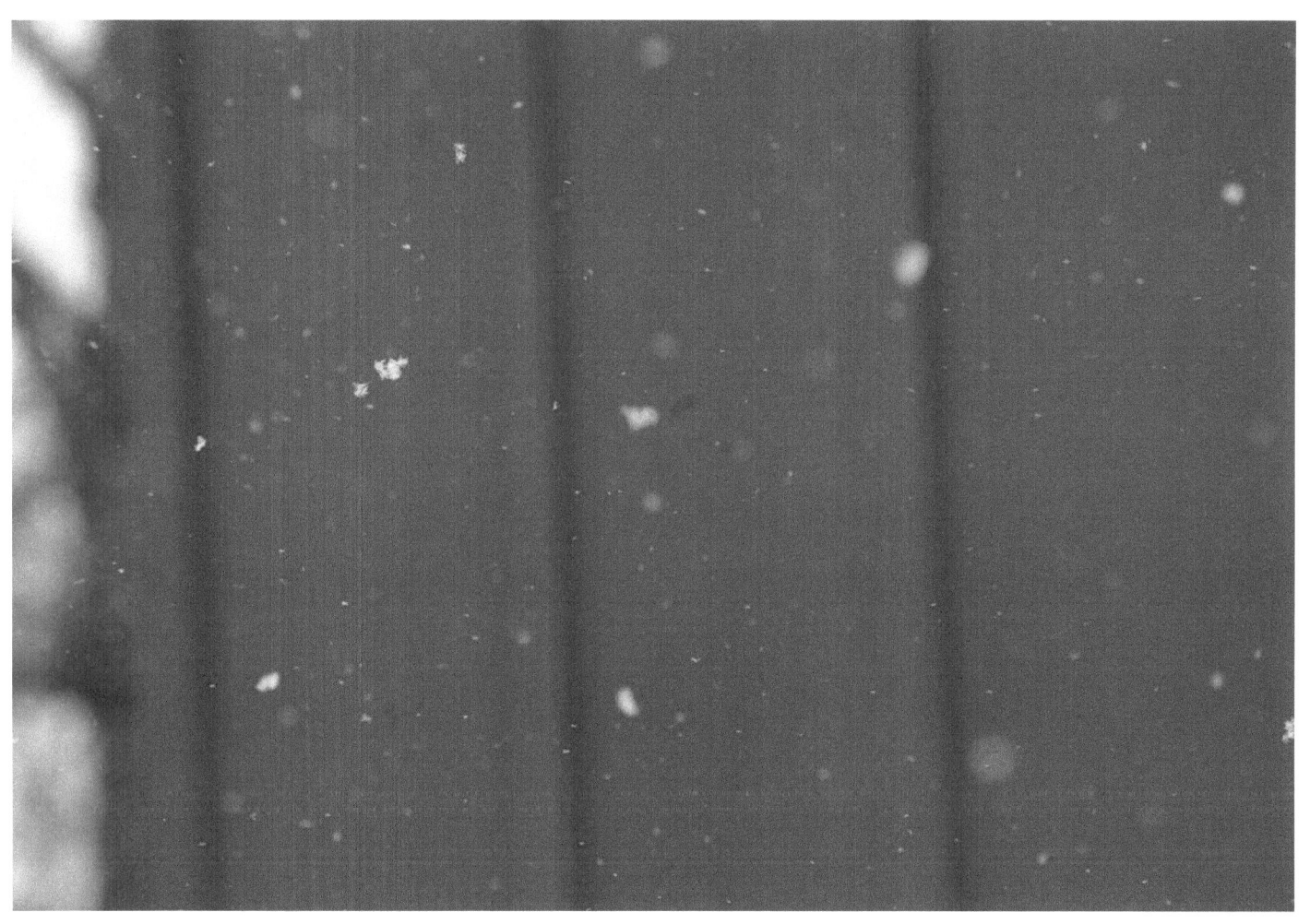

unique
like you and me –
snowflakes

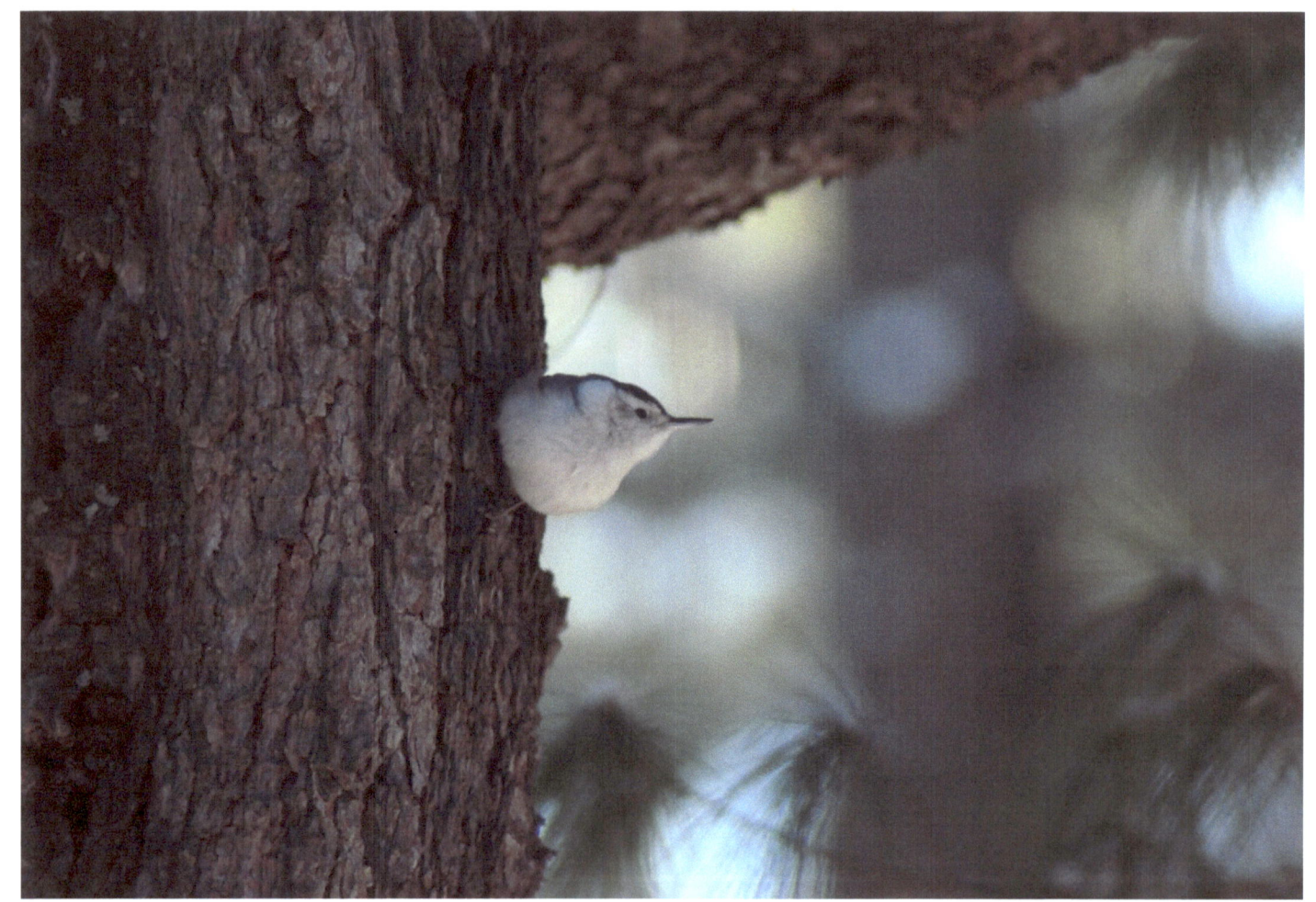

White-breasted Nuthatch

Nuthatch –
perpendicular to the tree
seemingly defying gravity

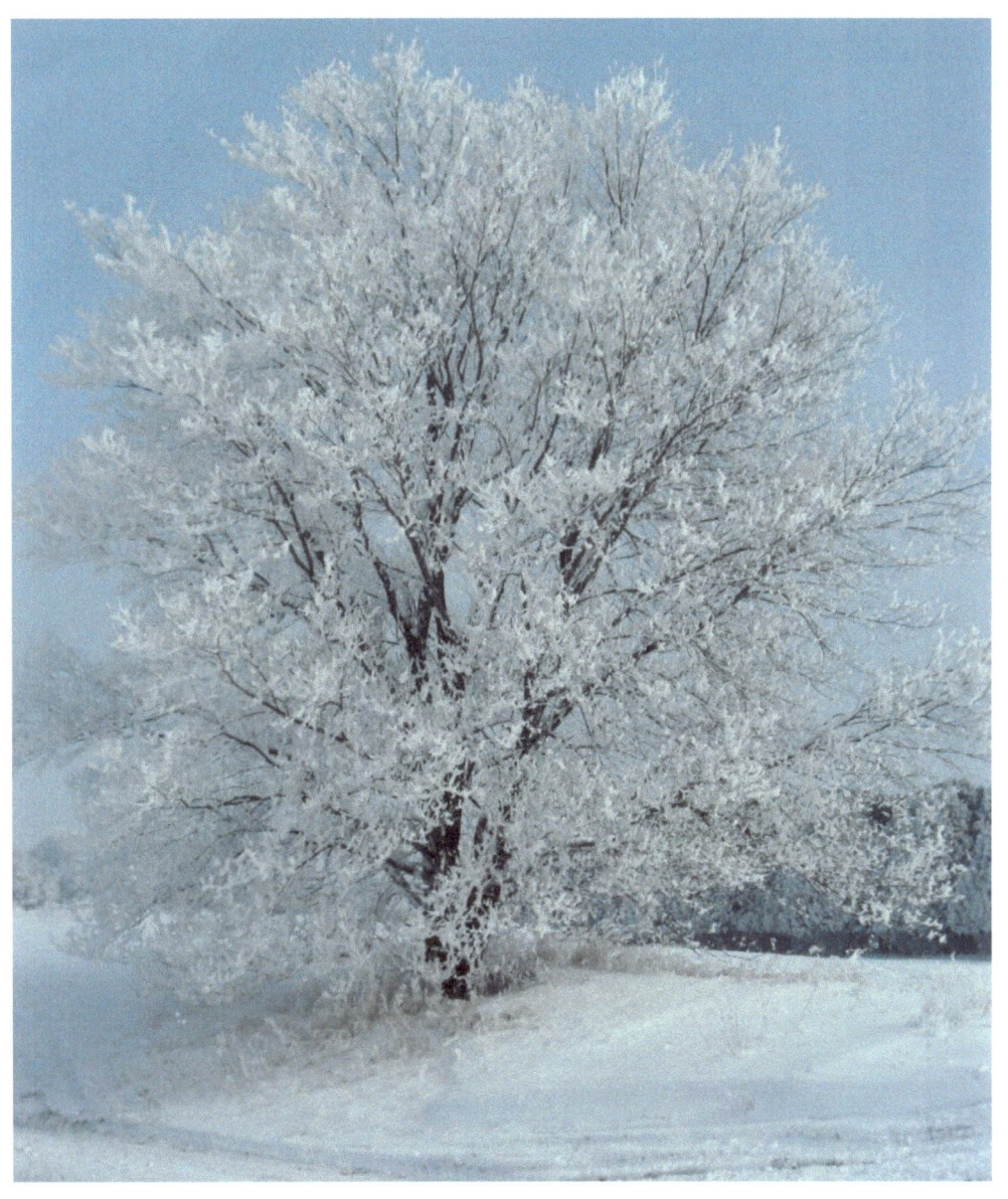

confectionary dream –
Jack Frost blew his breath
across the land

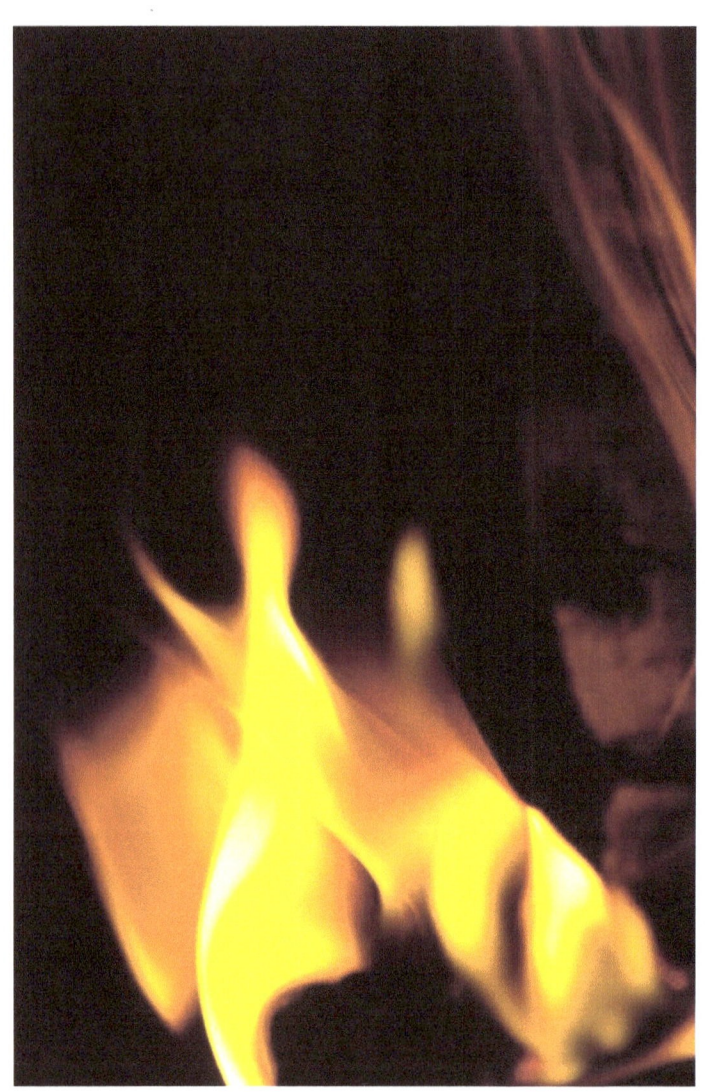

flickering flames
crackling wood
warmth –
snow falling
outside

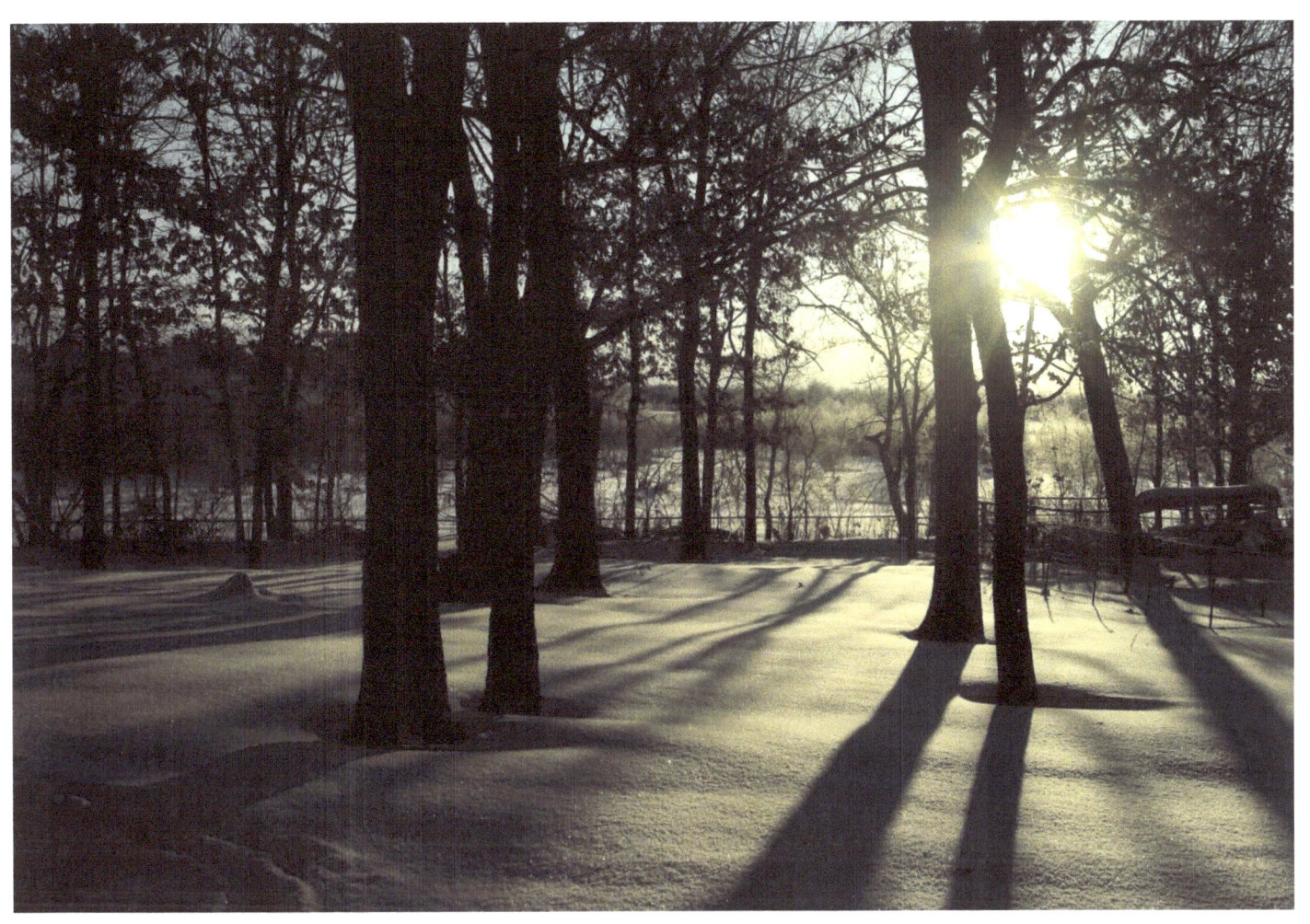

early morning tea –
vision of light and shadows
grace my backyard

Spring

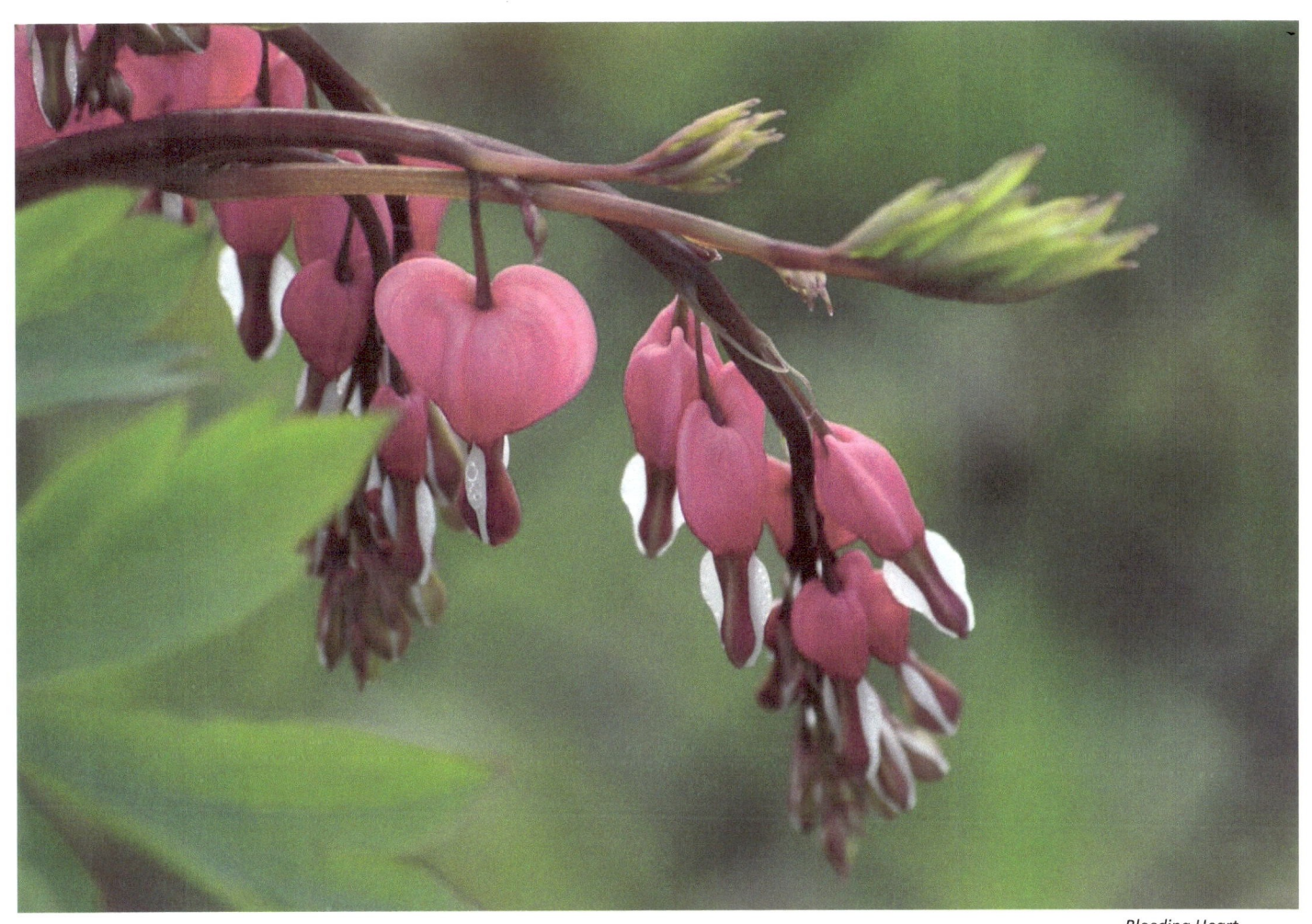

Bleeding Heart

no blood circulates
through these hearts
pulsating with life

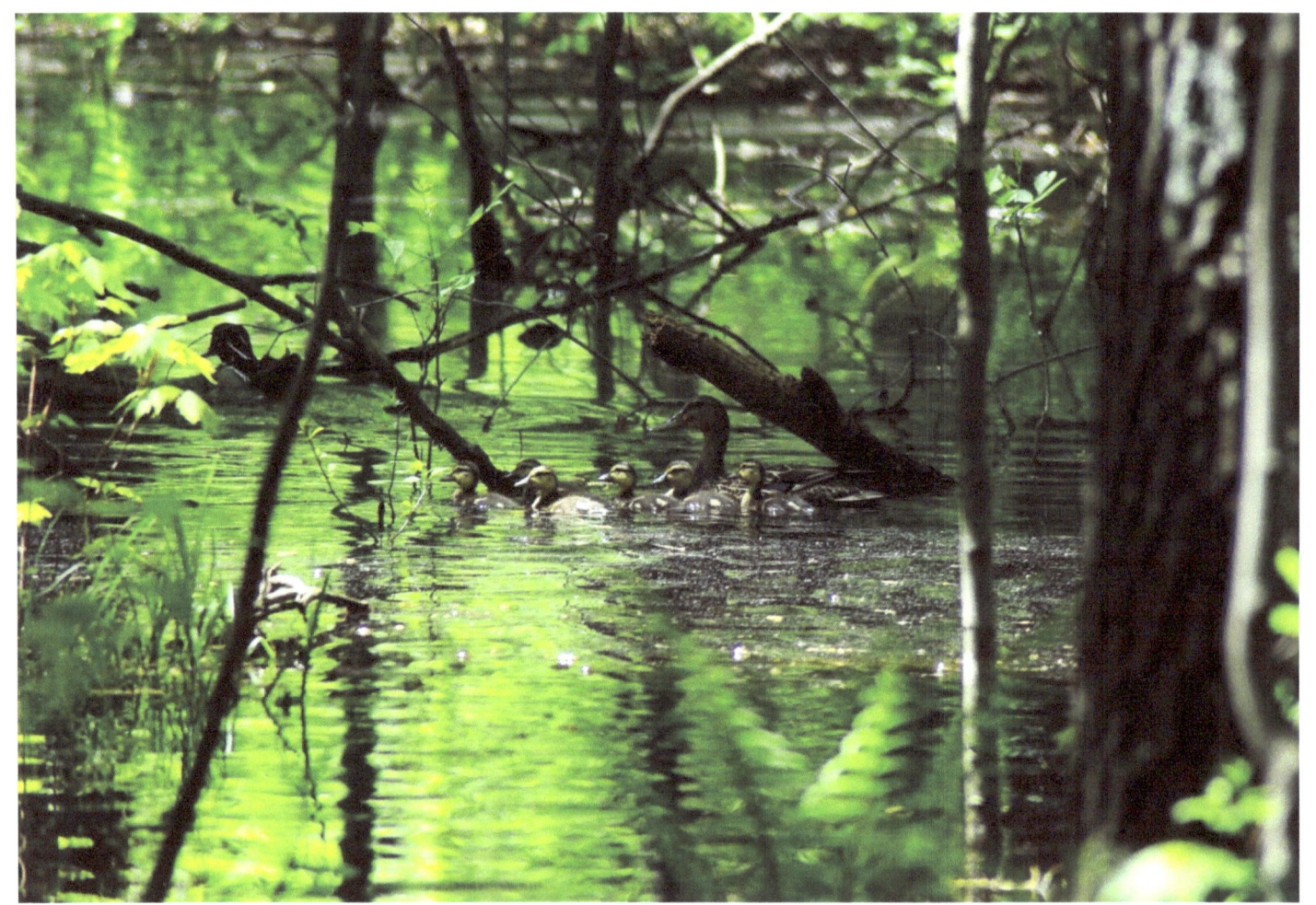

Wood Ducks

a watery woodlands –
a family
in a green canopy sea

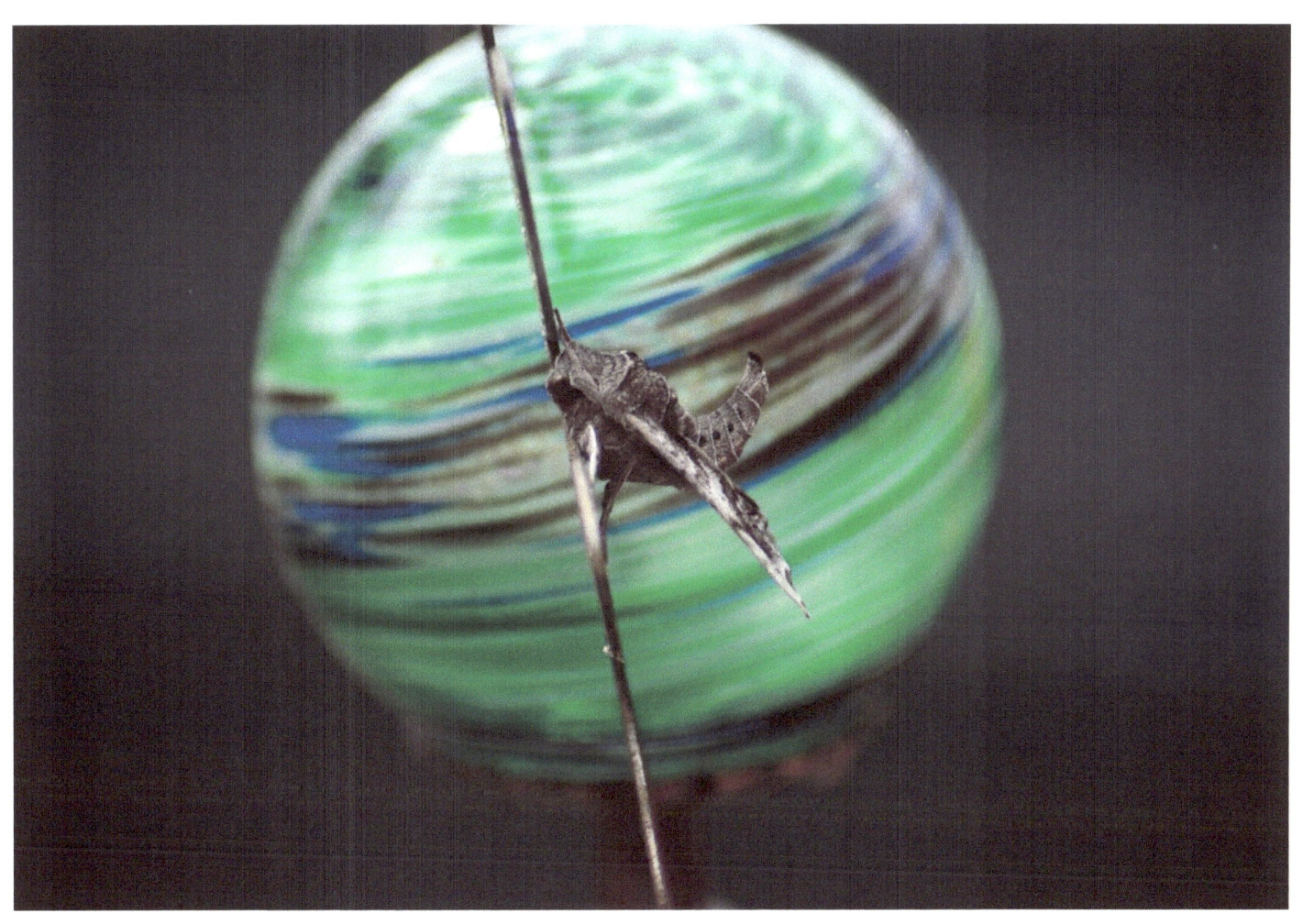

stellar beauty on earth –
moth

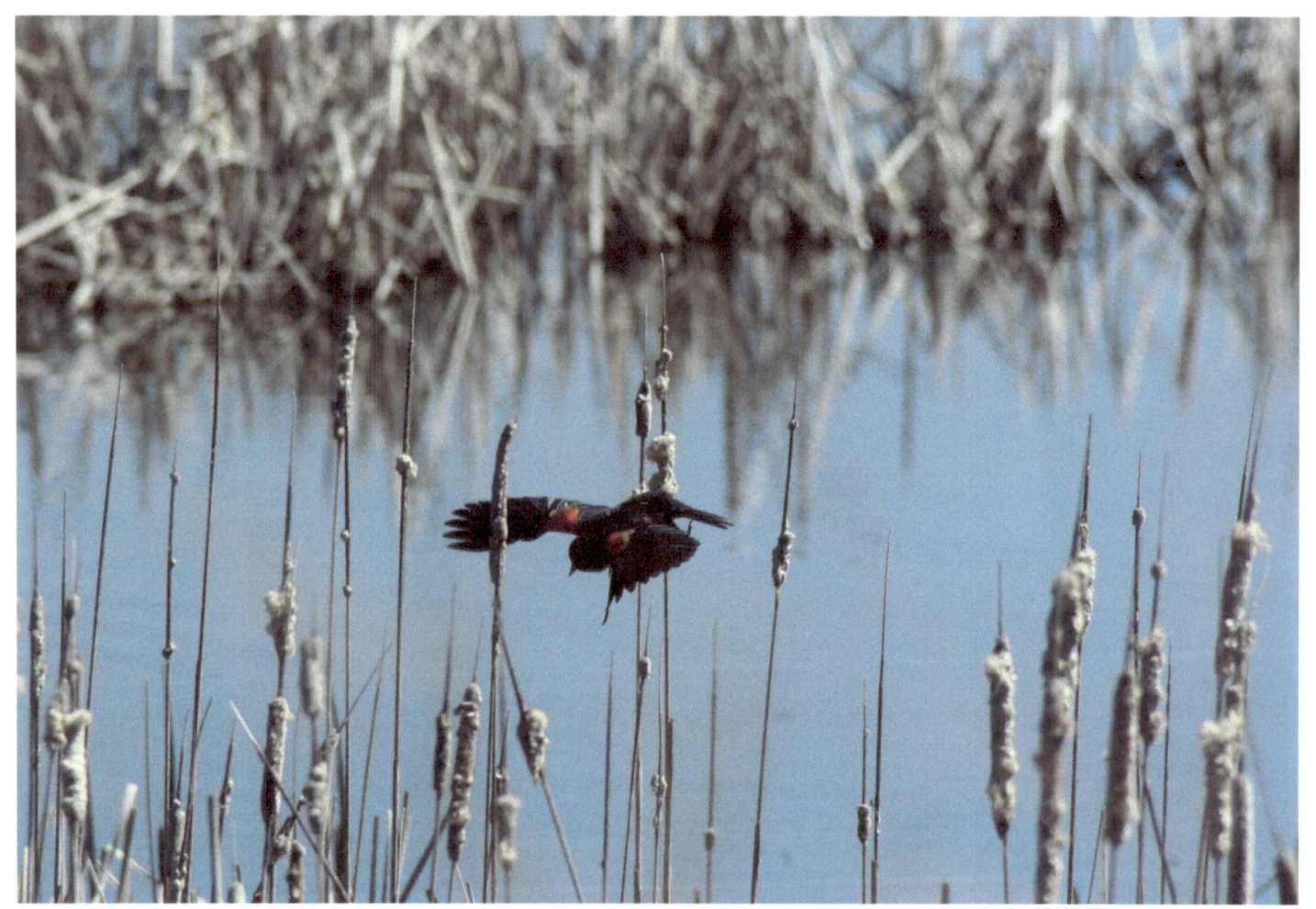

Red-winged Blackbird

like a ladies fan,
he unfurls
and flies away

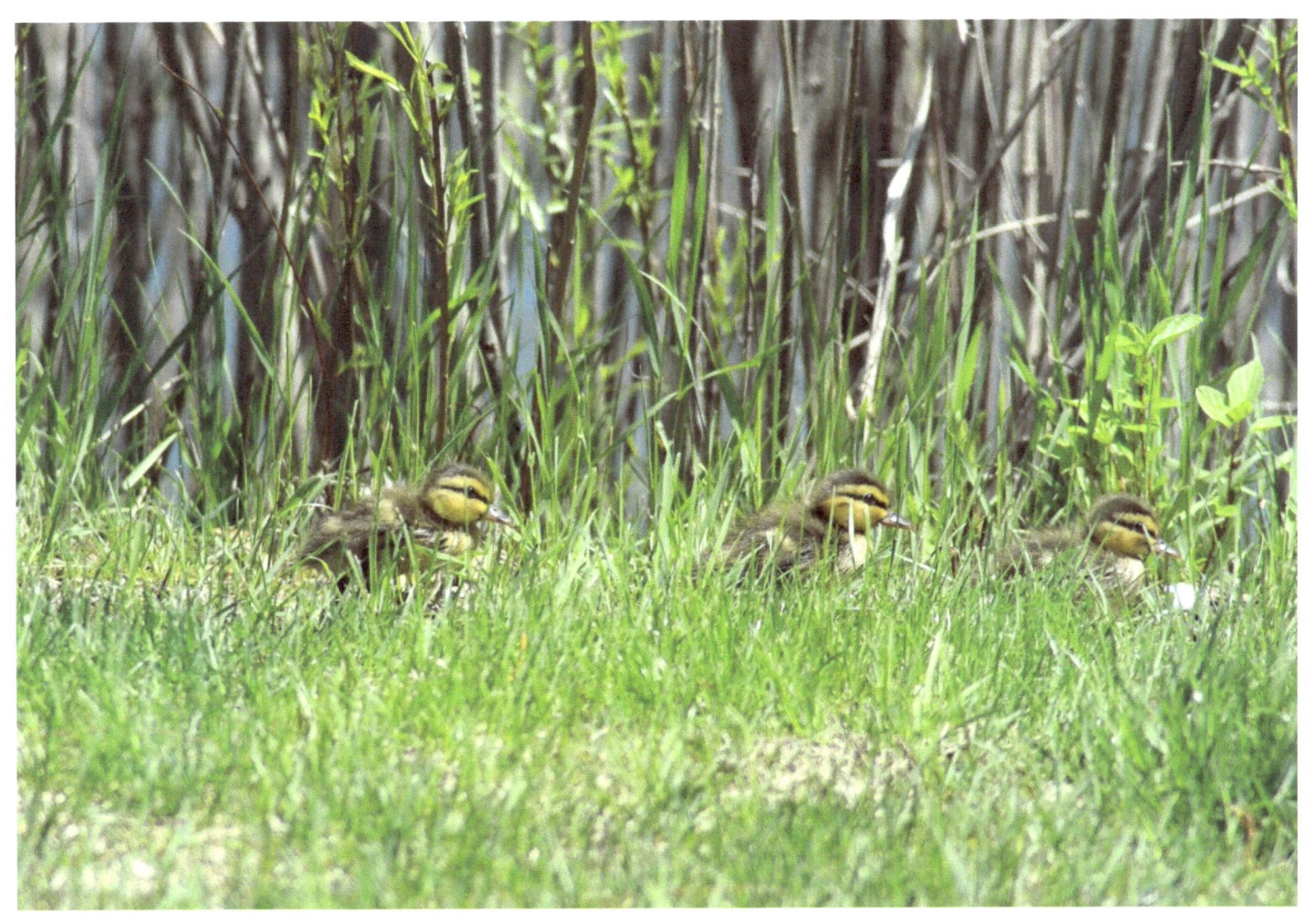

waddling
across my path -
new life

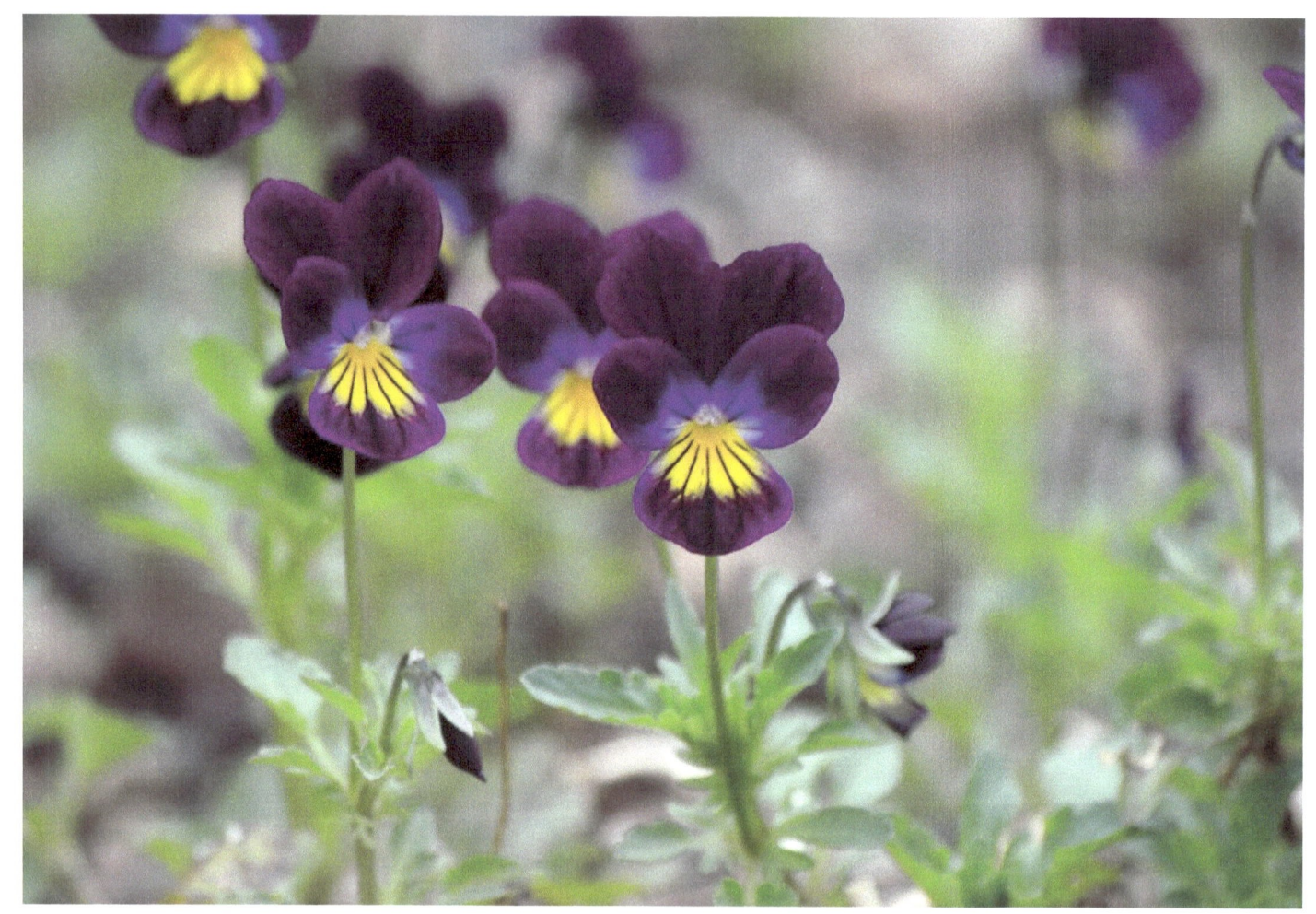

Johnny Jump-Ups

jumping up for joy –
their smiling faces
always turn my frowns around

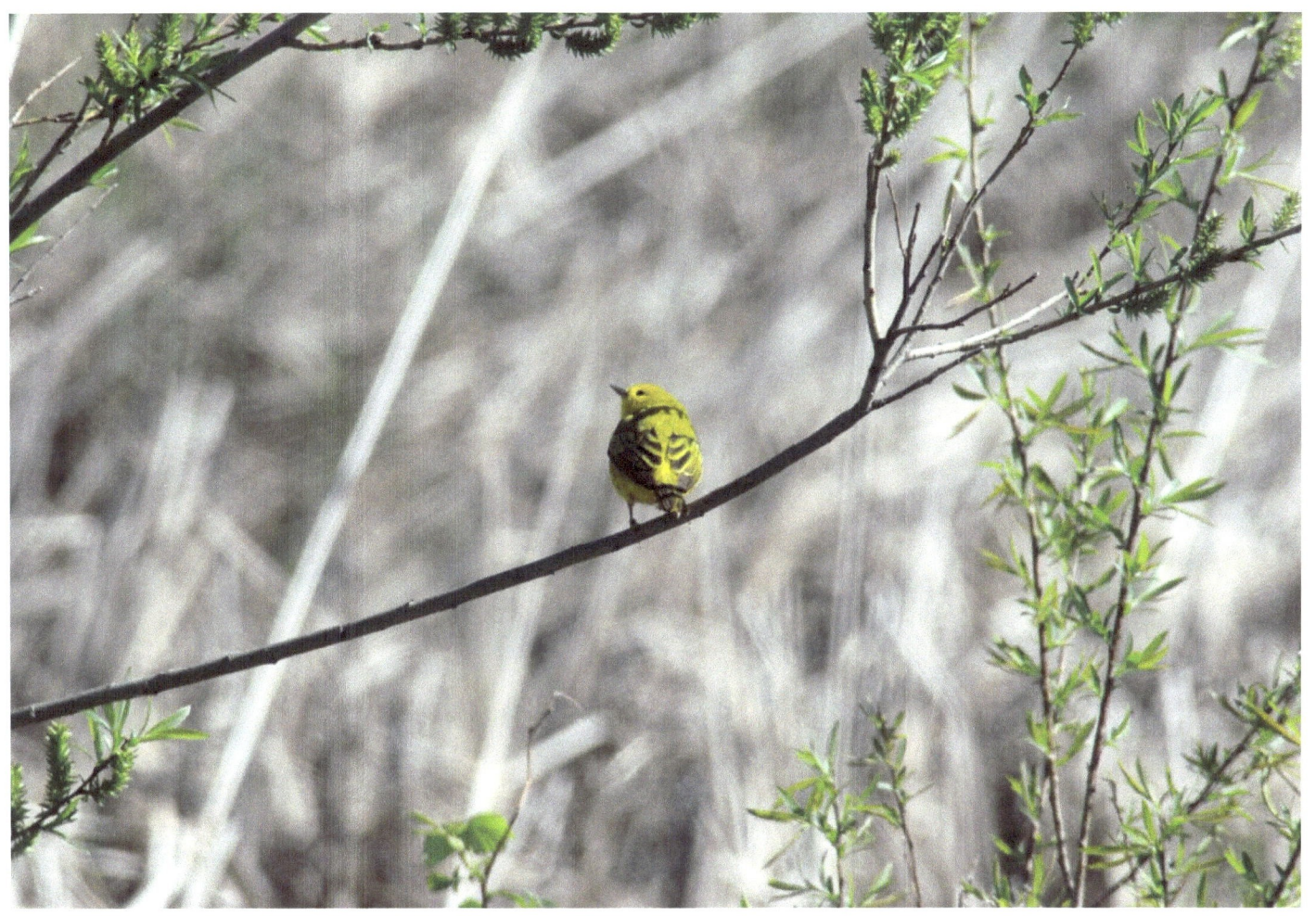

Yellow Warbler

sunshine yellow –
happiness in a small package

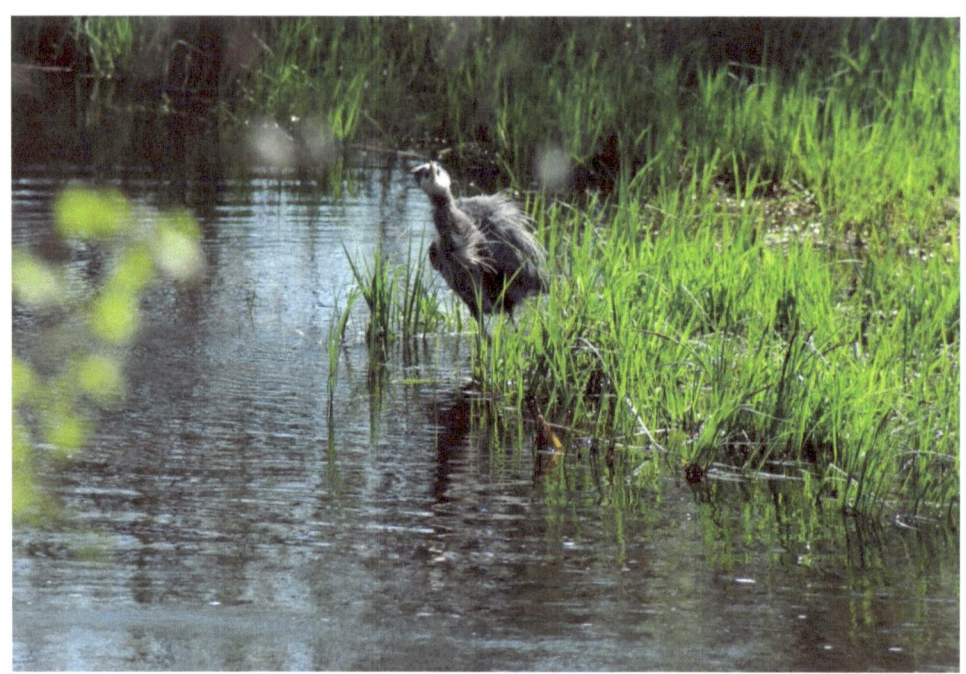

Great Blue Heron

shaking his withers
he looks like a clown
but every feather
falls into place
as he gracefully
saunters away.

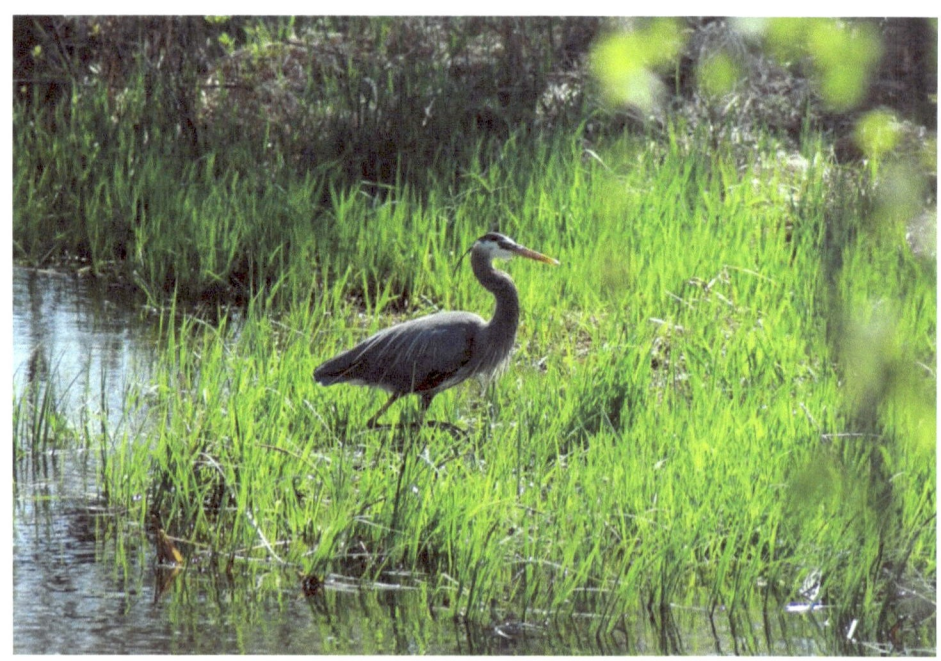

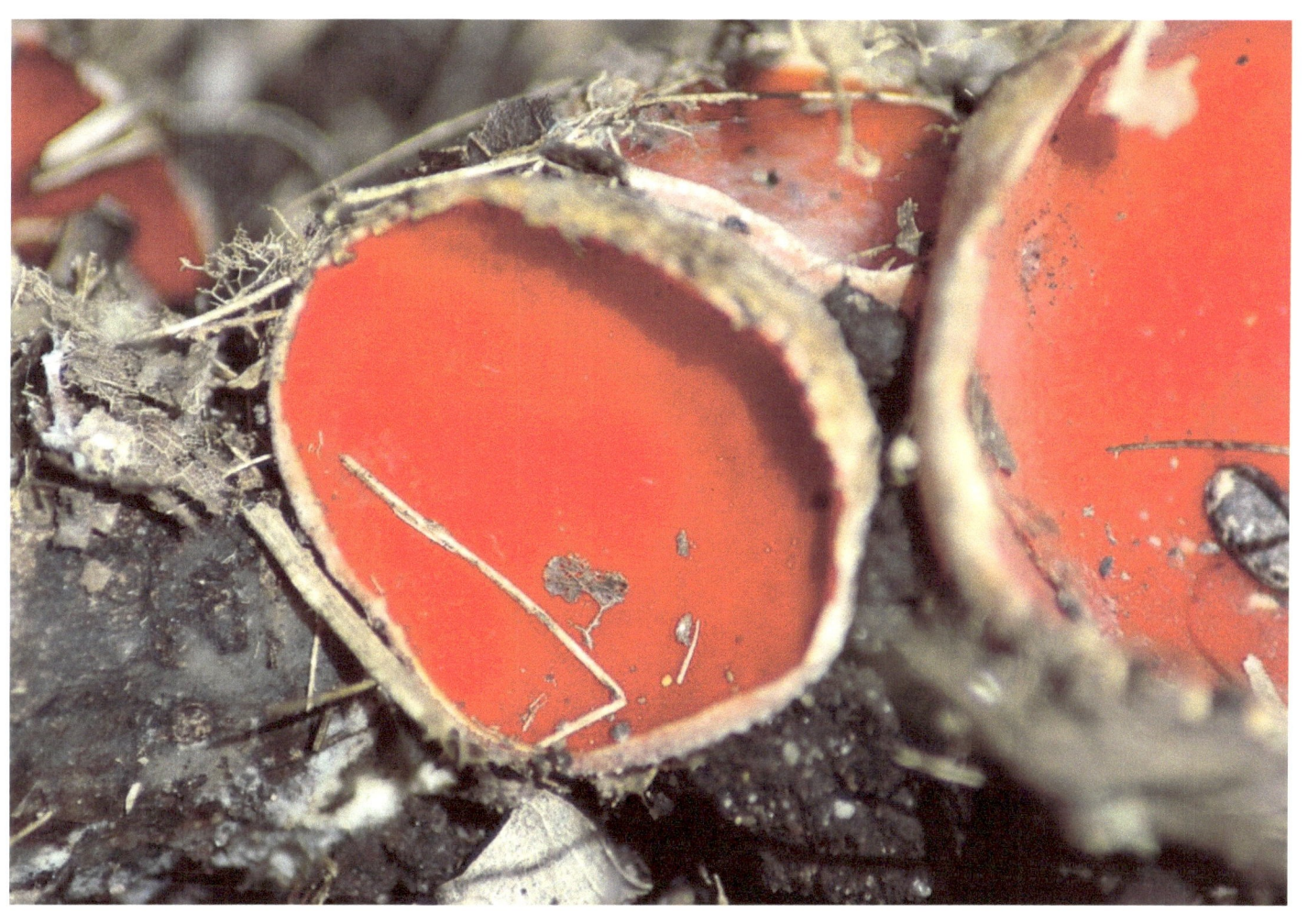

warnings flash
beneath withered leaves

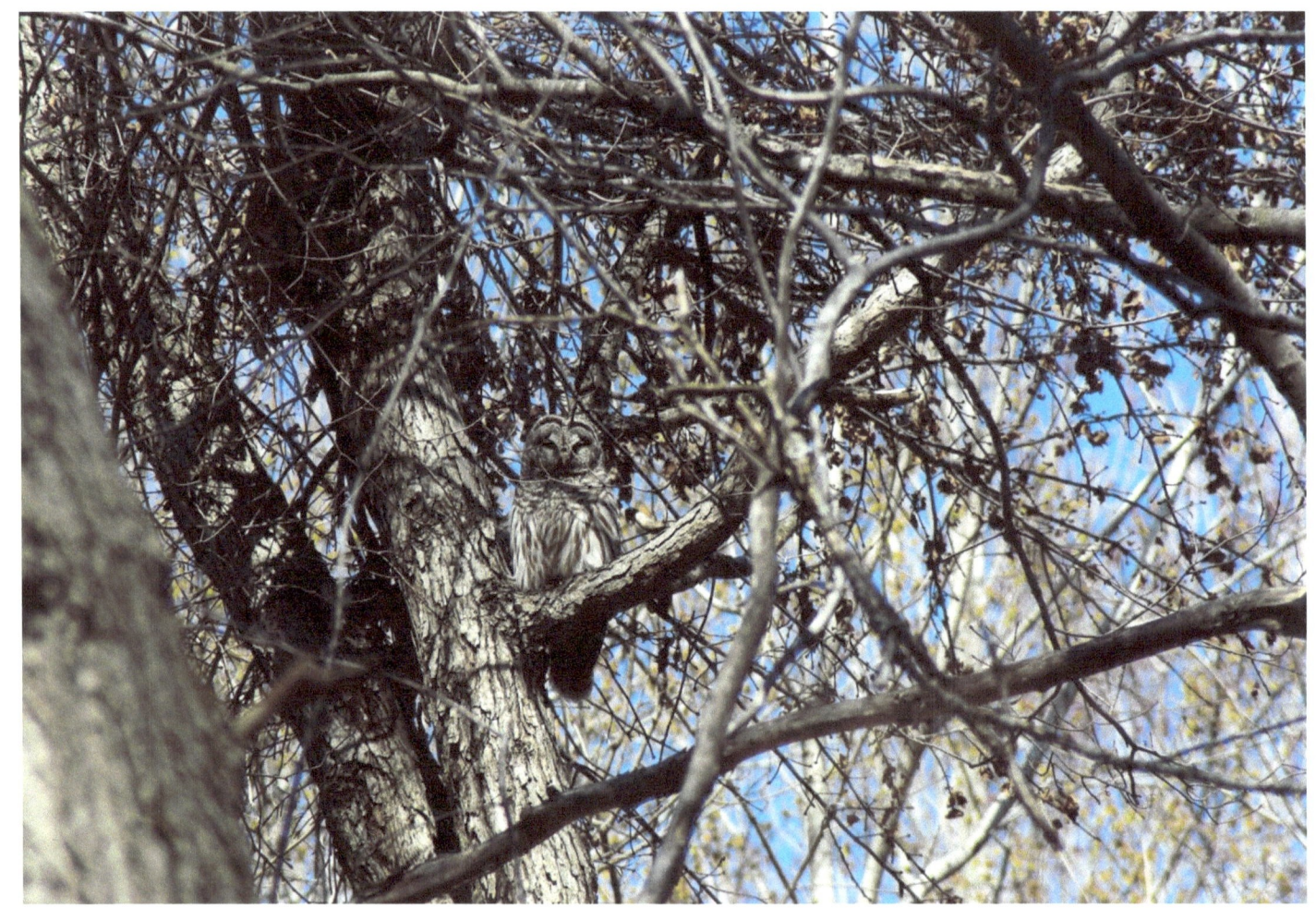

Barred Owl

Can you find me
sitting here?
I blend right in,
just the tree
and the wind.

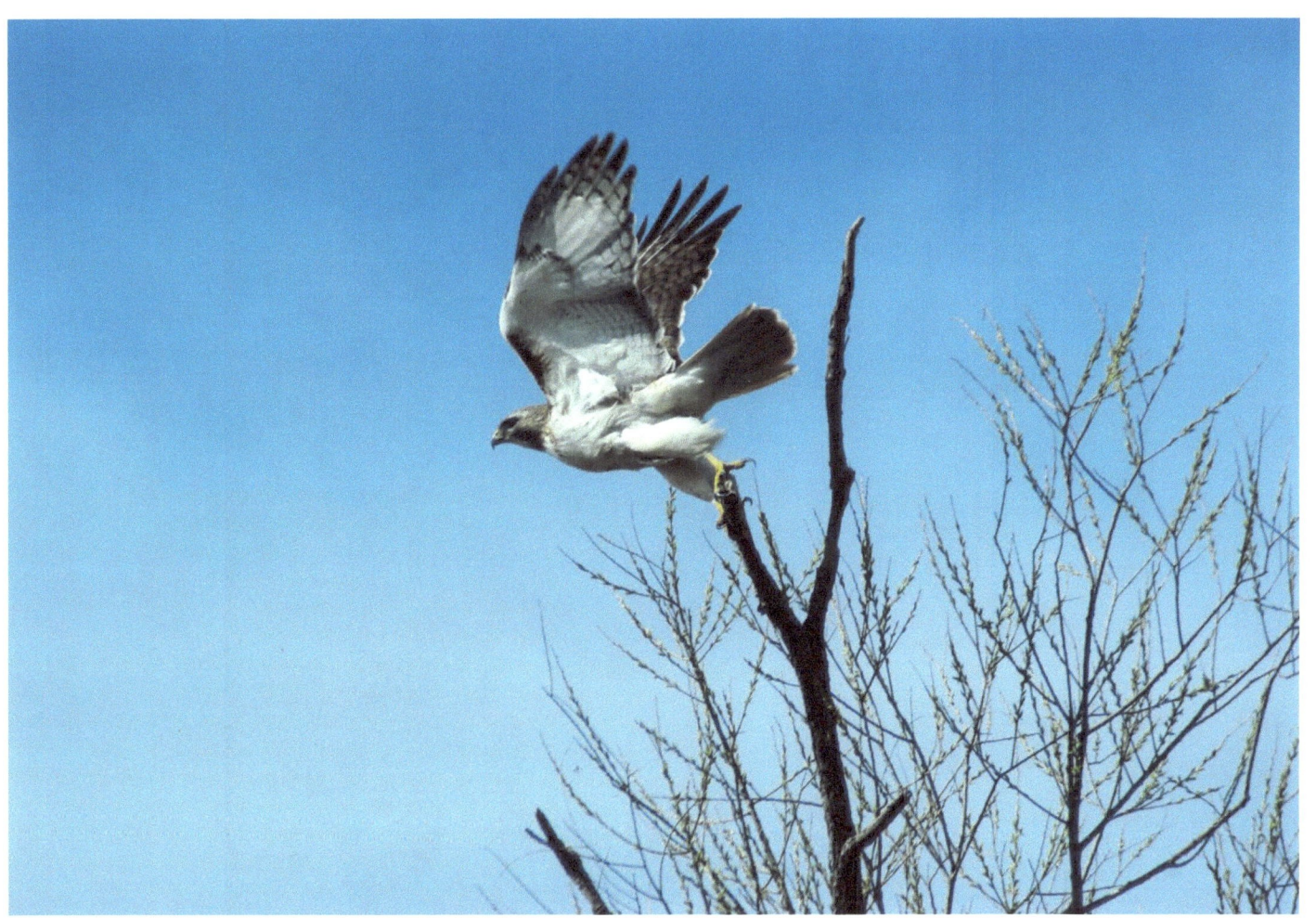

Red-tailed Hawk

muscles ripple with the feathers
as the hunter takes flight –
predator

chalk dusted moon -
a stencil in the sky

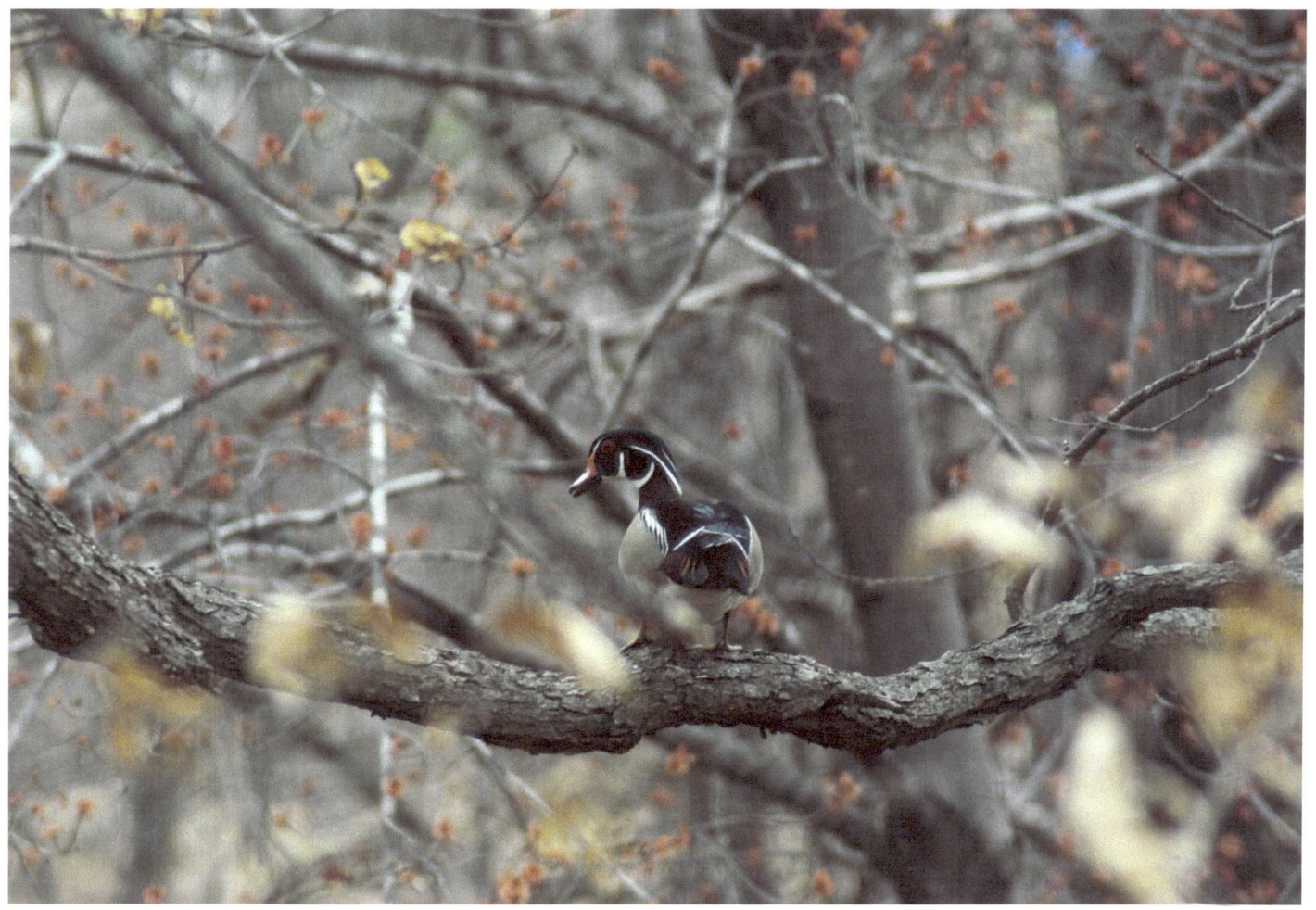

Wood Duck

a fancy ball, a masquerade
stopping by on his way home
not a wrinkle in sight

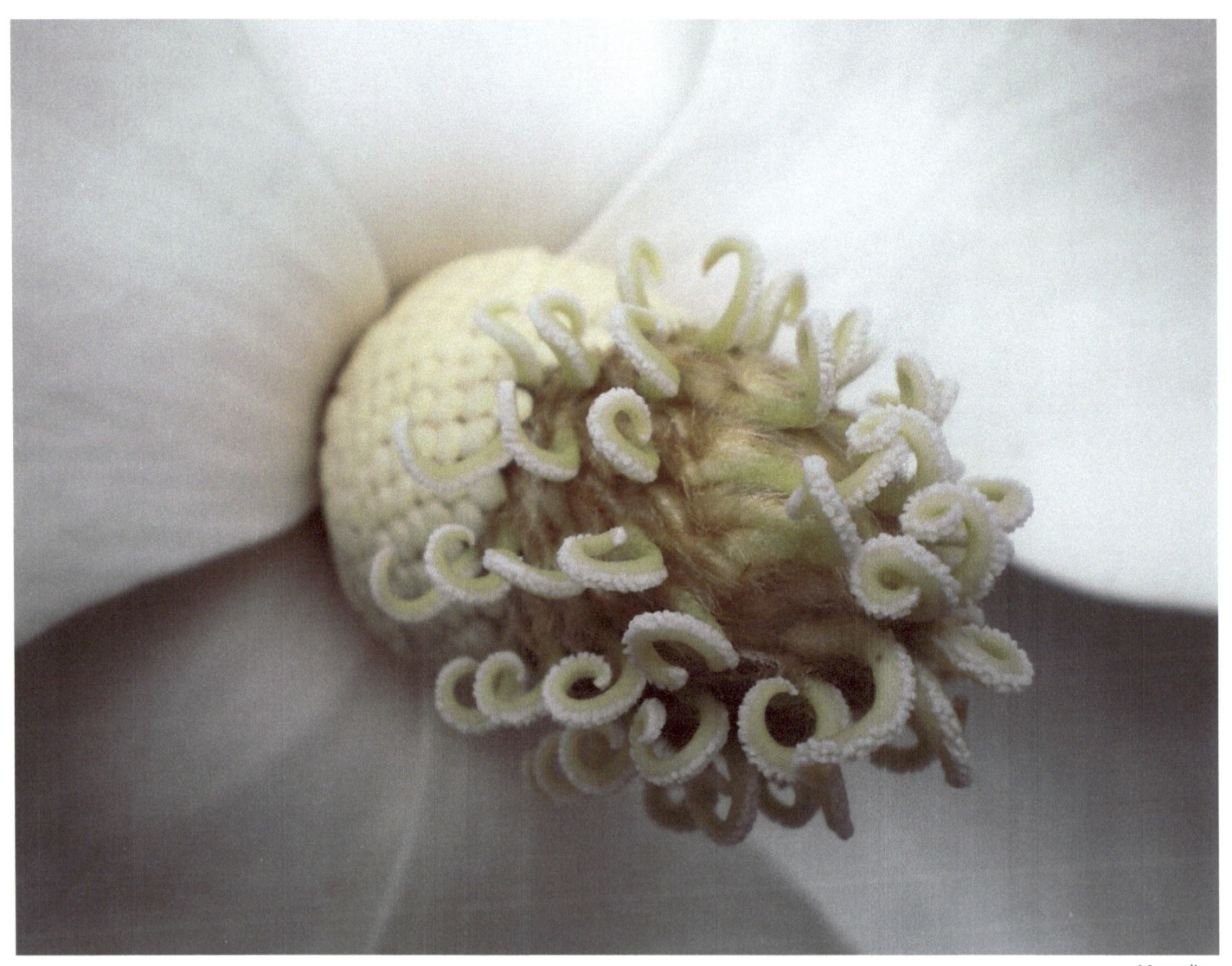

Magnolia

a bit of heaven -
pure white petals,
candied curly cues

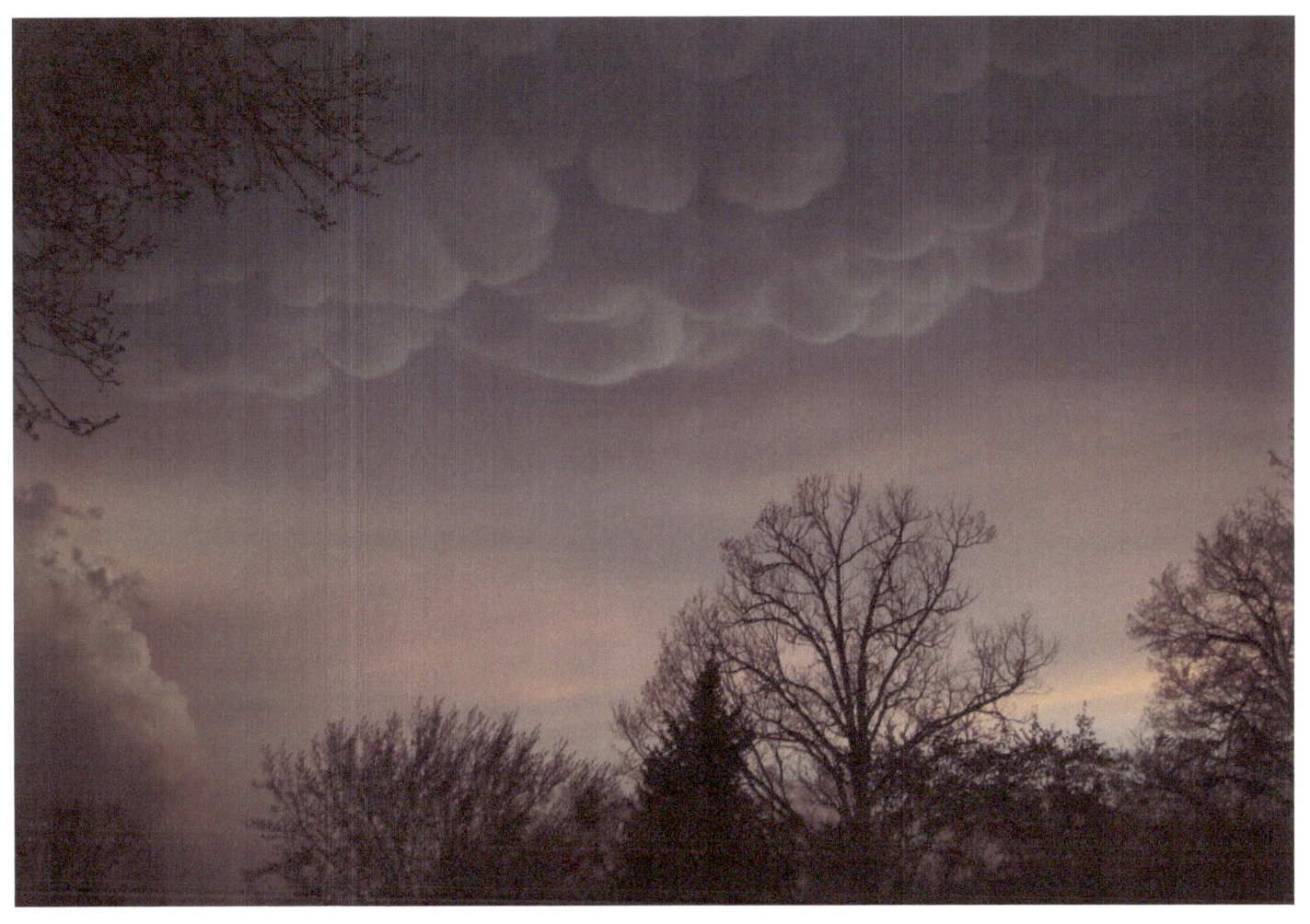

Mammatus Clouds -
the knuckles of heaven
reaching to earth

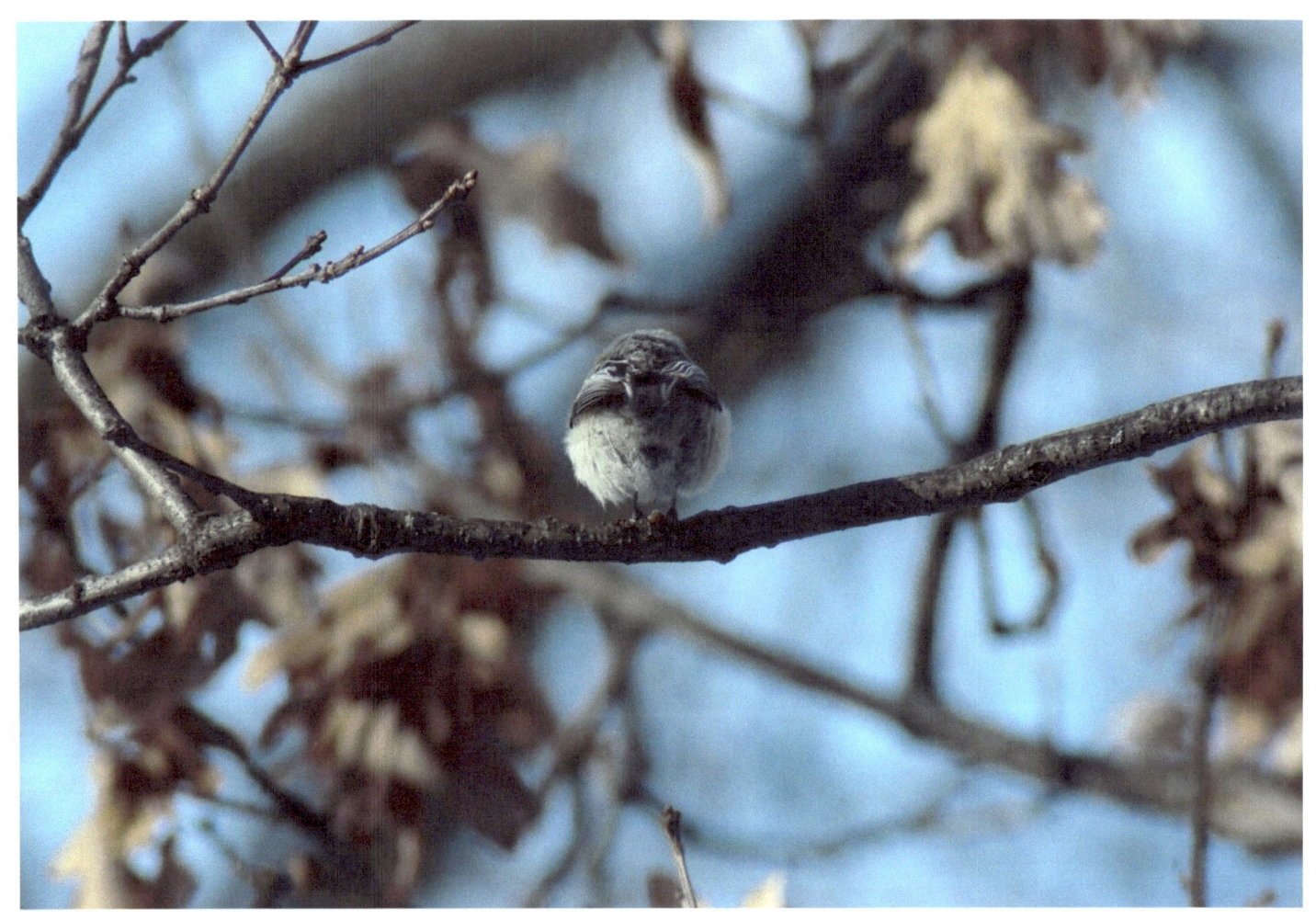

The End

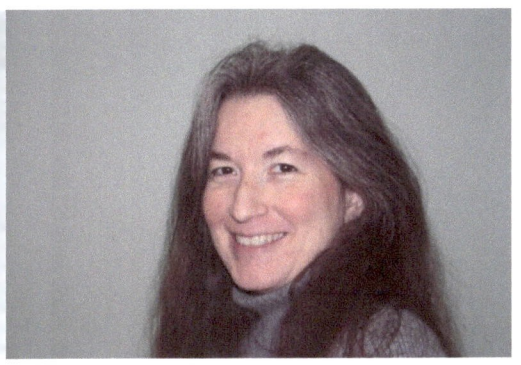

Michelle Hed is a photographer, poet and artist living in Minnesota. Michelle finds her art with every glance out her window and every step out her door. She is happiest when she is outside with a camera in her hand. Her poems have appeared in *A Handful of Stones*, *Haiga Online,* was a finalist in the *Poetic Asides Poem a Day Challenge 2009* and her photography has been awarded in local contests. She maintains a blog, The Pen, Lens and Brush, for all her artistic endeavors. She is married to her best friend, has two beautiful daughters and two mischievous hounds.

www.ingramcontent.com/pod-product-compliance
Lightning Source LLC
Chambersburg PA
CBHW050747180526
45159CB00003B/1375